Flowers for the Table

Flowers
for the
Table

Daphne Vagg

B.T. BATSFORD LTD. London

For John and the family, who bear with me

© Daphne Vagg 1983
First published 1983

ISBN 0 7134 4176 3

Filmset by Servis Filmsetting Ltd, Manchester
and printed in Great Britain by
The Anchor Press Ltd, Tiptree, Essex
for the publishers
B.T. Batsford Ltd
4 Fitzhardinge Street
London W1H 0AH

Contents

Acknowledgments

My special thanks are due to: my husband, John, who took many of the
photographs and did all the drawings; my family and friends who allowed me to
create havoc in their dining-rooms on photography days; those friends who so
kindly lent me their precious old books, photographs, china, linen, plants and
flowers; The National Association of Flower Arrangement Societies (NAFAS)
for permission to quote from their publications and to use photographs from
The Flower Arranger. The arrangements are by the author unless otherwise
acknowledged.

Preface

There is no place in the home where flowers are more welcome than in the dining-room. . . . Certain it is that when one comes into a breakfast room and finds it cheery with flowers, his mental mood responds and he is prepared pleasantly for the duties of the day. Flowers give added pleasure to every meal and the spirit of cheerfulness which they impart aids the digestion as well.
E.A. WHITE, The Principles of Flower Arrangement, 1926

lthough for centuries flowers in the hand have been regarded as a symbol of friendship (if one carried flowers it was not possible to draw a sword), it is only comparatively recently that flowers have become synonymous with hospitality and welcome to the table of one's host or hostess.

In this book I have taken 'flowers' as a collective term which includes not only flowers but foliage, seed heads, fruit, berries, vegetables and wood. Flower arrangement today embraces any kind of decorative display using plant materials, often with other components and accessories.

Students who come to flower arrangement classes at adult education centres or flower clubs almost always want to arrange a table decoration early in the course. It is usually for a birthday dinner or a wedding anniversary celebration or for Christmas or Easter. This can suggest that flowers are only for special occasions rather than for everyday. This comes I am sure, from the mistaken idea that flower arranging is expensive and therefore a luxury to be afforded only rarely. But nothing could be farther from the truth. A modicum of skill, a little forethought, an eye for colour and a surprisingly small quantity of flowers can produce an arrangement to enhance any table.

The book looks at the ways in which flowers have been used on tables in the past and offers practical suggestions for today in the hope that we shall not allow this attractive decorative custom to die out.

When we entertain, food and drink are important features, but good conversation and an attractively set table are surely important too. Perhaps I may be forgiven for repeating yet again an often quoted Persian poem because it is so especially apposite to table flowers:

If of thy mortal goods thou art bereft
And from thy slender store two loaves are left,
Sell one, and with the dole
Buy hyacinths, to feed the soul.

Daphne Vagg
Mole End, 1982

The sacred lotus of the
Goddess Isis laid over
food on an offering table
in Ancient Egypt (based
on a tomb painting)

CHAPTER 1

To Begin at the Beginning

Thou shalt prepare a table before me. . . .
23RD PSALM

Offering Tables of Ancient Egypt

gyptian tomb paintings of more than 3,000 years ago show us the earliest glimpses of tables bearing food and decorated with flowers. Diners at that time were apparently offered small, individual flat-topped tables supported by a central leg or tripod. The sacred blue lotus of the Nile, emblem of the Goddess Isis, was laid singly, or in bunches, over piles of food, including grapes, figs, pomegranates and vegetables, wild fowl and fish.

The lotus was probably more an offering than pure decoration; it was there to placate the Goddess and to protect the diner against misfortune and evil.

Ancient Rome

During the Ancient Greek and Roman classical civilizations flowers were widely used for garlands, chaplets and circlets and particularly for strewing in the streets, on floors and beds and even on meal tables on ceremonial occasions.

The Romans' evening meal was often referred to as 'the hour of the roses' and in Emperor Nero's 'Golden House' (*c.* AD 37–68) 'the supper rooms were vaulted and compartments of the ceiling, inlaid with ivory, were made to revolve and scatter flowers'. Later Lampridius records that the Emperor Heliogabalus in the third century AD installed a reversible ceiling in his palace which released violets and other flowers in such profusion that, on one disastrous occasion, some of his guests lost their lives because they were unable to free themselves from the weight of the blossoms!

The popular Victorian painter, Sir Lawrence Alma Tadema, used this theme for his painting 'The Roses of Heliogabalus', and captures the abandon and excesses of decadent Rome.

Virgil (70–19 BC) describes autumn fruits so vividly we see them almost as a table decoration, not just as food: 'There are waxen plums of autumn's season and chestnuts and sweetly blushing apples; there is Ceres' pure gift, with love and Bacchus, there are blood-red mulberries with grapes in heavy clusters, and from its stalk hangs the blue-grey melon.'

9

'The Roses of Heliogabalus', by Sir Lawrence Alma Tadema, portrays the surfeit of flowers at feasts in Ancient Rome (*Sotheby's*)

The Renaissance

Although a number of fourteenth- and fifteenth-century Italian paintings show banquets in progress with considerable details of table appointments, I have found no evidence of flowers used as decoration on the tables.

In the religious paintings and altarpieces of this time flowers and plants are usually included for symbolic purposes, but in secular paintings it is reasonable to suppose that the scenes portrayed were fairly true to life. In paintings of banquets there may be pots of growing plants such as carnations nearby or bay and box trained and clipped, topiary fashion, into spherical and open ring shapes. But there are no flowers on the lavishly spread tables.

Seventeenth-century Holland

We know that the splendid flowerpieces of the great seventeenth-century Dutch and Flemish painters never really existed as arrangements and were composed from notebook sketches made through the seasons. But what of the studies found in still-life paintings such as the banquet and breakfast pieces, in this case, quite literally, flower decorations on meal tables? Although the arrangement of food, utensils and flowers may have been subject to artist's licence, they would probably have been similar to those used at meal times. The flower arrangements look authentic. Far from being grand display pieces, they are rather simple little bunches which we can well imagine in a Dutch house.

Clara Peeters (1589–c.1657) included flowers in a few of her still-life paintings and the example in the Ashmolean Museum, Oxford, shows a white pottery urn holding an arrangement of roses, a tulip and a pink, martagon lilies, columbines, cornflowers, borage and pansies. It stands on a wooden table with a basket of fruit, a glass of wine, a pewter plate with nuts and cherries and a tazza of grapes. It could be the dessert course of a meal. The tulip may be a little out of place among the summer flowers yet the little arrangement looks as though it might actually have graced a table. One of Jan Soreau's still-life paintings in the same museum shows a little glass vase of columbines, roses and rosemary beside two much more important fruit arrangements.

A pottery vase of mixed flowers is included in Clara Peeters' seventeenth-century table-piece. (*Ashmolean Museum*)

Jan Soreau, who worked in Holland between 1615 and 1638, painted a delicate little glass vase of roses and aquilegias with his still life of fruit. (*Ashmolean Museum*)

Eighteenth-century Elegance and Splendour

In the middle of the eighteenth century in Europe we begin to find the phrase *surtout de table* being used when tables and table decorations are mentioned. Meaning literally 'above all', the *surtout* was an elaborate table centre-piece for important dinners and banquets.

It usually took the form of a *plateau* or base tray, often with a pierced gallery edging, with a central monument or temple, candelabra and statuettes of nymphs, military or classical figures and animals. One of the most famous is at Apsley House, London, and was presented to the First Duke of Wellington by Portugal in 1816. This massive silver *surtout* is 26 feet long and three and a half feet wide! A painting by William Salter shows this service in use at a Waterloo Banquet in 1836, with the statuettes holding floral garlands; and the Victoria and Albert Museum booklet on the Wellington Plate records that this was intended by the original designer, Sequeira. Sometime after the death of the First Duke, the use of real flowers was abandoned and the nymphs were given their original head garlands to carry instead.

On a less grand scale than the *surtout*, the epergne, or table centre-piece, was coming into fashion. In the eighteenth century this was usually an elaborate silver branching stand with low bowls or baskets to hold fruits or sweetmeats. Not until later do flowers seem to have been used. Fruit was also frequently piled high in pyramids on a fruit dish or tazza – a wide, shallow bowl on a high stem or plinth which was often part of a dessert service.

In Williamsburg, Virginia, USA, a large part of the town has been preserved and restored to its eighteenth-century colonial glory, attracting many tourists and sightseers. The present-day arrangers there try, as far as possible, to re-create the atmosphere of two centuries ago, using mainly fruit and foliage for

Some of the nymphs on a magnificent candelabra from the Wellington Plate looking curiously bereft without their intended floral garlands. Other pieces from the same Plate can be seen on page 27 (*Victoria and Albert Museum*)

13

their table decorations. In Virginia, as in England, in the eighteenth century, for principal meals there might be a first course of sweets, then a main dish, followed by a third dessert course after the table-cloth had been removed. Pyramids of fruit in eighteenth-century style are often made at Williamsburg on wooden cones spiked all over with headless nails on which apples, oranges or lemons are impaled with evergreens filling the spaces between.

ARTIFICIAL FLOWERS

In France, and in England too, sugar confectionery was much used for table decoration and often entire garden scenes with decorative trees, low hedges and parterres were made from sugar. In fact, the whole emphasis of eighteenth-century decoration was on the use of artificial, rather than natural, materials.

R.P. Brotherston, writing in 1906, records the 'depraved practice' of the eighteenth century in substituting for natural flowers those made of paper, silk and other materials. These were considered prettier and more genteel! A contemporary remarks on tables being decorated 'with all the foolish mimicry of art in painted leaves and paper flowers'.

A Meissen eighteenth-century floral table centre in porcelain, enamel and ormolu, 58 cm (23 in.) wide. (*Christie's*)

Later in the same century a chronicler records at the Lord Mayor's dinner how the piles of sweetmeats had disappeared 'to make way for the city plate and artificial flowers'. The Meissen porcelain factory produced the floral centre-piece shown here. Each flower is exquisitely wrought but its artificiality is never in doubt. The skill of the confectioner, silversmith, or artist in porcelain or paper was apparently preferred to that of the gardener or florist.

A TOUCH OF NATURALISM

There is a charming description, in Anne Hughes's *Diary of a Farmer's Wife 1796–1797*, of preparations for a party at a fairly well-to-do farmer's house; 'Jan. ye 26. . . . Mistress Prue and her sister did cum earlie to help lay the table with my best dammy [?damask] cloth and they did fill little pottes with box and holly, Mistress Prue saying all the qualitie do do so; so I very pleased thereby.'

The reference may not be strictly authentic, but was certainly based on a diary written in the last years of the eighteenth century and has the right feel. It sums up very neatly the way in which the fashions of royalty are handed down to 'the qualitie' and then to the middle-class and so on as the years go by.

But it took something of a revolution, in the middle of the nineteenth century in Victorian England, to bring fresh flowers in profusion onto the tables at meal-times. This came about when it became fashionable, and later commonplace, to dine *à la Russe*.

CHAPTER 2

The Heyday of Table Decoration

So it was that when we began to think of decorating our dinner-tables with flowers – the time is well within my recollection – we passed successively under the tyranny of the three-tier glass tazza, the pools of looking glass, the fountains, the blocks of ice; the elaborate patterns of leaves and flowers on the table-cloth and the centres of bright coloured damasks and brocades. We have been of late somewhat under the dominion of the shallow pool of water. . . .
GERTRUDE JEKYLL, *Flower Decoration in the House*, 1907

After 1850

For several hundred years it had been customary in England to put all the fish, meat and game dishes on the table with the vegetables and sauces at the beginning of the meal. As the meal progressed the empty and dirty dishes accumulated until the dessert course was reached. The tablecloth (invariably white, though occasionally with a coloured border) was then removed or 'drawn' and everything was cleared away. The dessert dishes and finger bowls were then set out and the meal resumed without the white cloth.

The introduction of *diner à la Russe* from the Continent where it had already found favour meant that the servants handed round and cleared away each course in turn. In this way it became unnecessary to 'draw' the cloth and it was then possible to dress the table more elaborately with floral centre-pieces. The very phrase has a Victorian ring. In no time at all fashionable hostesses were vying with each other to present more and more elaborate and expensive table decorations. In grand houses the head gardener and his staff may have been responsible for these decorations; in hotels and banqueting rooms, a professional florist was employed. In more modest homes, the lady of the house might take on this 'agreeable task' herself.

So began the heyday of floral table decorations. They became, by the end of the century, overwhelming, cluttered, costly even for those days, gimmicky and what we would now call 'in poor taste'. But flowers on the table were enjoyed as never before. Flowers, ferns, foliages and fruits abounded in profusion for more than half a century, calling forth admiration, wonder and

A 'March Stand tastefully arranged with Flowers, Ferns and Grasses'. (From *Domestic Floriculture* published by W. Blackwood & Sons, 1874)

16

envy among rival hostesses and not a few derisory comments from both men and women writers.

The Essence of Victoriana

To our present-day eyes the Victorian tables look overdone. But the pictures that have come down to us are mostly of grand occasions and such ostentation would not have been equalled in the smaller home. However, the general effect of table decoration is usually of a bower of ferns and greenery interspersed with brightly coloured flowers. There was invariably a centre-piece, either an epergne or a March stand, flanked by at least two other epergnes or vases and possibly many more, trails of leaves, ferns or smilax weaving between candelabra and serving dishes and even between place-settings. Looped garlands of foliage decorated the table skirt with little posies at intervals

A very elaborate design for a dinner table from the catalogue of a Parisian florist, 1900

Something of the atmosphere of a Victorian dessert course is re-created with a period epergne and dessert service on a bare polished table

wherever there was a space. Menu-holders often incorporated a small container for flowers as well. Wire frames and arches were sometimes used to carry greenery or floral decorations down the centre of the table.

FLOWERS AND FOLIAGE

Ferns were acknowledged favourites, because of the vogue for growing ferns in conservatories, grottoes, shrubberies and indoors in Wardian cases. Maidenhair fern was perhaps the most popular, though 'asparagus fern' ran it a close second. Smilax was the first choice for looping and twining over the white damask cloths, although ivies, clematis, Virginia creeper and rose foliage were also used. Geranium leaves were used, overlapping, to create patterns on the cloth.

For formal dinners flowers were likely to be roses, carnations, orchids, chrysanthemums, stephanotis, eucharist lilies, sweet peas and lilies-of-the-valley. Mignonette was a firm favourite as a 'filler', in much the same way that arrangers today use *Alchemilla mollis*, but mignonette had the bonus of being sweetly scented.

18

Selaginella and lycopodium are frequently mentioned, yet seldom used for flower arrangements today. They are club mosses of various kinds with long trailing stems. *Tweedia caerulea*, a small pale blue flower and *Francoa ramosa* (bridal wreath) in pale pink and white were also much used but are far less common today. The emphasis for table decoration was clearly on greenhouse and conservatory plants when these could be home-grown or afforded at the florist's.

Fruit was generally arranged separately from the flowers, either in the lower dishes of epergnes and stands, or on separate dessert dishes.

A present-day table with flowers in the Victorian manner

ONE COLOUR AND ONE FLOWER EVENTS

Mrs De Salis in her *Floral Decorations* published in 1891, describes in detail (what a pity there are no pictures) dinners and luncheons based on one colour or one flower, which were the height of fashion at that time. So, one might have a pink or yellow, green or gold dinner or a lavender, orchid, forget-me-not or foliage table, and there are three suggestions for primrose dinners. Under the title 'Autumnal and Winter Season Dinners' she gives this description:

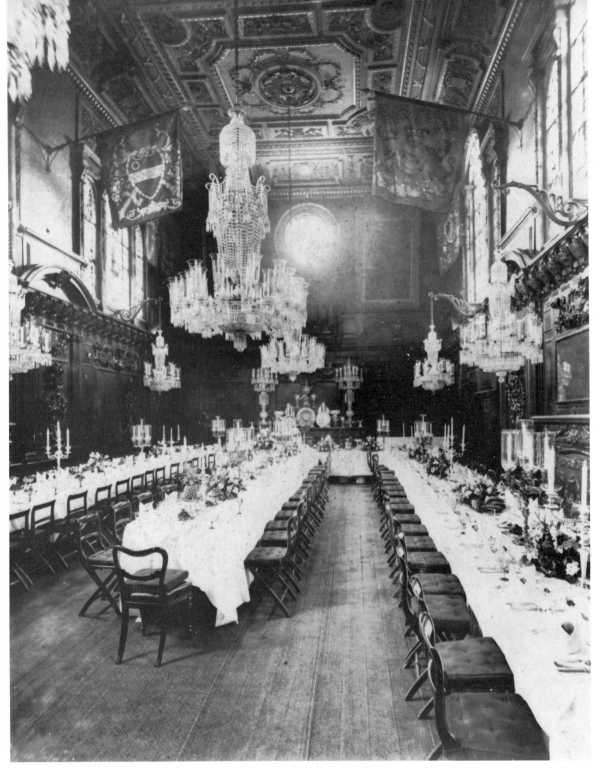

A banquet at the Mercers' Hall in London in the 1890s. The decorative use of flowers and fruit is restrained for the period. (*The Worshipful Company of Mercers*)

Smilax used in loops and garlands on an Edwardian table (From *The Art of the Table* by C. Herman Senn)

A mound of red Virginia creeper leaves laid upon paper crumpled up in the form of a mound, in which the smallest of lights should be cunningly hid, is very charming. These lights may be little wicks, floating in oil, in glass dishes the size of a florin. They should be so arranged that nothing except the tiny light or flame should be visible, shining out like glowworms between the leaves. Around this mound small wire trelliswork arches should stand, their height about eight inches, in which clematis might twine in and out. Down the sides of the table silver bowls filled with rowan berries, larger bowls of the same being placed top and bottom. Scattered about the table little quaint Dresden china figures should be placed, holding baskets of bonbons. Four silver candelabra make a good light for such a table. The guest cards tambourines and the menus small yachts, the bill of fare being written on the sails.

How tastes change. What would we think nowadays about glowing mounds of leaves, wire arches, yachts, tambourines and Dresden figures all on one table? What would the local Fire Prevention Officer think of it as a hazard? Mrs De Salis has noted many 'charming' ideas, such as *sacs de fleurs* made of brocaded satin or plush in the shape of a reticule with cords and tassels, which has an inner receptacle of tin to place the flowers in; or a Sedan chair, entirely covered with yellow narcissus, the poles ornamented with pale blue satin ribbon; or even 'a table of water lilies and grasses . . . with a great block of ice in the centre and miniature glass bowls with small gold fish in them, placed around it'!

Edwardian Taste

King Edward VII and his Queen, Alexandra, did much to lighten the heavily ornate preferences of later Victoriana. The influence of Art Nouveau and oriental styles meant a less florid approach both to the arts and interior decor, including flower arrangement. The hallmark of the Edwardian attitude to flowers was that they should be 'in good taste'. Throughout 'the long summer' which preceded the First World War flowers on the table took on a lighter, more airy look, with less heavy greenery and flowers packed in less tightly.

King Edward VII was said to favour sweet peas and R.F. Felton writes in 1910. . . . 'A table of Sweet Peas, which owing to its success I have had to repeat three times for the King's birthday dinner at St James's Palace, was composed of masses of sweet peas in bowls of various heights . . .'. The same writer describes other table decorations which he had found successful, such as low bowls of dark wallflowers with salmon-pink tulips; daffodils with sprays of yellow jasmine and 'brown ivy sprays on the table'; pale yellow chrysanthemums with small pale mauve Michaelmas daisies and yellow or bronze autumn leaves; and at Christmas time, mistletoe with orchids and lily-of-the-valley with a light design of small pieces of mistletoe on the cloth.

An elaborate table for a wedding breakfast at the turn of the century. (From *The Art of the Table* by C. Herman Senn)

FANTASTIC TABLE SETTINGS

In spite of the Edwardian emphasis on good taste, some extraordinary table decorations were thought up and carried out for wealthy clients at the Savoy Hotel and elsewhere, which quite put the Victorian fountains, glass lakes and blocks of ice in the shade.

Mr George Kessler held a dinner in a floating gondola on a lake created in the Savoy Hotel courtyard. Carnations and white roses (with the inevitable loops of smilax) decorated both the gondola and the table, under a white silk gauze canopy similarly decked with flowers. In 1910, at the Trades Hall, Leicester, four 7·5 metre (24 feet) diameter clock faces served as dining-tables for a clockmaker's dinner. At each 'hour' stood a tall glass vase of flowers.

Dining-rooms were transformed into the North Pole; farm-yards; a coach meet with real turf, roads and small trees; a golf-course; a mining camp; a roulette table with all the flowers in red because it was on *rouge* that the host's fortune had been won. Best of all, perhaps, was the luncheon in the lion's den with four full-sized lions roaming at will. The obligatory white damask cloth, even here, was garlanded with smilax.

GERTRUDE JEKYLL

Known primarily as a gardener and garden designer who worked with Sir Edwin Lutyens, the architect, Gertrude Jekyll wrote *Flower Decoration in the House* in 1907. Miss Jekyll's table pieces would not look out of place today. She loved to create two complementary groupings, one high and one low, for

A table decoration for a dinner *à la Russe* in 1909 – according to Mrs Beeton

example: daffodils in a tall glass vase and tulips in a low bowl; white iris and artichoke leaves in a tall glass with white stocks and grey-leaved stachys in a shallow dish, or a tall jar with a low basket beside it and foliage trailing across and over the table edge. Her arrangements have much of the quality of still life paintings rather than the romantic trailing and fussy frothing that we associate with Victoriana.

After World War I

History tends to record the life-style of the rich and important. We do not get to know as much about the man in the street and his way of life and whether or not his wife arranged flowers. What is certain is that the fashions of the well-to-do appear further down the social ladder many years after and continue for 20, 30 years or more.

After the 1914–18 War, however, some of this changed. Books and magazines were in more plentiful supply and were read by a larger cross-section of the community. The artistic gap between the rich, the middle-class and the working-class was beginning to narrow and flowers on the table became more common in the average home.

In 1918, F.M. Ramsay in his *Everybody's Flower Book* wrote:

There are very, very few dwelling-places now where flowers are not sometimes set in the living-room . . . the use of white damask seems to me to be like the custom of decorating our tables with flowers, worthy of being perpetual. There is a great charm about well-polished mahogany and other woods but . . . they do accentuate the spotty effect which is always difficult to avoid on a dinner table.

He continues with an idea we might copy today: 'If you wish to show the wood during dinner, I think the old-fashioned slips going along each side under the plates preferable to a mat for each plate.'

Among his suggestions for tables are a bronze statuette with scarlet geraniums or red holly berries; lustres with white flowers and light green foliages; wild scabious and mauve-pink thrift with silverweed leaves. For containers: little white pots, custard glasses, deep-coloured glass finger bowls, black Wedgwood bowls and blue Nankin china. His suggestions generally are inexpensive and available to almost everyone. Ribbons matching the colour of the china (he does not say how they were used) were favoured and marble figurines in summer. Carnations, poppies, ferns, the berries of holly, ivy, privet, cape gooseberries, old man's beard, montbretia and honesty pleased him – and Bonsai trees. Fruit, he felt, was somewhat neglected and he recommended his readers to use 'red strawberries, rosy peaches and nectarines, golden apricots, pineapples or oranges, pears and apples in many shades of red and russet and so down the gamut to the deep brown nuts'.

A wedding buffet table at home. Summer garden flowers in mixed colours are
arranged in a white cherub container. Small posies decorate the swagged cloth

Blue, pink and white flowers decorate a black table laid with blue and white place mats and pink napkins. The neutral-colour china allows many decorative variations

The black table is dramatically emphasized by the use of black and white only. The arrangement of orchids, tulips and carnations is not particularly modern in itself but the overall effect is far from traditional

Using the picture on the wall for inspiration, a modern arrangement of black painted cane, stems and leaves with pink gerberas makes a good talking point

Tan, brown and black with frankly artificial roses create a different mood

Four versions of the same table with the same china

The 1920s

In the 1920s, Mrs Beeton was warning readers against a table being too heavy or overcrowded with flowers, so presumably the Victorian influence was still quite strong. Even her own recommendation we would find overpowering today:

> For a table laid for say, six to twelve guests, two to four flower vases or bowls, around which trails of asparagus fern, smilax, etc. are draped, four candlesticks and half a dozen small silver dishes containing bon-bons, almonds and preserved fruits will be ample decoration.

She advocated flower-heads floating in wide shallow bowls of crystal, coloured glass or pottery or black Wedgwood with a brightly coloured bird, dragonfly or butterfly fastened to the edge of the bowl (photograph below).

Her principal piece of advice is not to have too many flowers of too many different colours, and to arrange them naturally with delicate wavy grasses or fern fronds. Bulbs grown in brightly coloured or black china and earthenware bowls; Autumn leaves, bracken and berries; bowls of Spring primroses and cowslips or Summer grasses with water-lilies; all found favour at this time.

At the end of the 1920s, Anne Lamplugh wrote *Flower and Vase* about the flowers she arranged in her own home throughout the months of the year. Her arrangements are simple, never ostentatious and with real feeling for form, colour and texture. She was writing in an era when oak furniture was most popular and small mats had taken the place of a white table-cloth. She follows

Roses floating in a bowl with a kingfisher ornament, of the type popular in the late 1920s and 1930s

A present-day arrangement evoking the 1920s' style

in the Gertrude Jekyll tradition, suggesting a pewter tankard flanked by two pewter plates as the basis for a variety of table pieces. Brilliant scarlet geraniums with a few of their leaves are one suggestion; also tulips, laburnum, peonies, phlox, marigolds and roses. Taller stems are arranged in the tankard and one or two flower heads and leaves float in the plates. As alternative containers she suggests a terra cotta pitcher and two honey jars, or grouping two silver candlesticks on either side of a silver bowl or ebony candlesticks (so typical of the 1930s) with a black Wedgwood bowl. Anne Lamplugh suggests matching the candles to the flowers and today's arranger could carry on these simple practical ideas.

The 1930s

In 1934, Constance Spry published *Flower Decoration* and, in the words of Sir William Lawrence's preface to it, she 'precipitated an aesthetic renaissance'. Her name was to become synonymous with flower arrangement even in homes

which did not aspire to be artistic. It was not so much a renaissance as a complete break with the Victorian and Edwardian styles and the unwritten rules that went with them. Mrs Spry did not want rules but simply to open people's eyes to the decorative possibilities of all kinds of plant material from lichened branches to cabbages. She delighted in colour and texture, garden and wayside flowers and leaves, vegetables and fruits.

She stated firmly her 'belief that no general principle can be laid down for table decorations . . . The only way to deal with it, given your table and surroundings is to use your imagination . . . and not be limited by any preconceived idea'. She could create masterpieces with red roses heaped like a cushion in an alabaster bowl, with elderflowers stripped of their leaves, with rhubarb shot up into flower or brilliant nasturtiums trailing from a sea shell. We do not all possess her gift but we can cast aside preconceived ideas. The advice is as sound today as it ever was.

Constance Spry putting the finishing touches to the Queen's table at a State banquet at Lancaster House, London in 1953. (*Photo kindly lent by Mrs Dora Buckingham*)

The 1950s and After

Constance Spry was not alone. Gardeners, especially women, who loved their flowers, sought ways of arranging them more attractively. They grouped together and formed clubs; the clubs eventually formed a national association and in 1959 the National Association of Flower Arrangement Societies (NAFAS) was born. Its growth was phenomenal and today there are 90,000 members in its 1,250 clubs. Flower arrangement has truly come to everyone.

CHAPTER 3

Table Flowers Today

It is the table that will be the cynosure of all eyes, and it is the integration of all its components which will give the greatest degree of decorative success . . . it is really of primary importance to treat the table as a unit on its own, . . . it is on this that the attention will be focussed.
CONSTANCE SPRY, *Party Flowers*, 1955

n several of her books on flower decoration, Constance Spry stressed the importance of an overall style, or quality, as she calls it, in which cloth or table surface, china, cutlery, linen and flowers are united and integrated. This should always be the first consideration. It is not so much the style of the room, though this can give a valuable lead, it is the style of the table itself, its appointments and the occasion or meal for which it is being decorated that are most important.

Most people live for many years in the same house with the same dining-table in the same room (though it may be redecorated from time to time) and often with the same china and linen as well for at least a number of years. It would be dull in the extreme if the flower arrangements on the table were always the same. Luckily there are many things which do change: the food, the time of day and therefore the lighting; the seasons and with them the flowers and leaves available; the occasion; the number of people who will be at the meal and whether it is formal or informal. We should make use of these changes to give variety to table decorations so that no one gets bored with the same old vase or bowl holding the same old type of flower arrangement year in, year out.

THE LONG, LOW TABLE ARRANGEMENT

It is hard to say just when the long, low, almost oval table arrangement began to make its appearance. Certainly, it was well established in the 1960s and almost as obligatory as the epergne was to the Victorians.

It evolved from the need to make a flower arrangement suitable for smaller dining-tables where plates and serving dishes had to be passed to and fro because there were no servants to wait at table. An epergne would almost certainly have been knocked over. Since the hostess in the average home was also the cook she could not spare time for lavish and elaborate flower arranging

The long, low table arrangement of today

except for very special occasions. The low arrangement remains a sensible and practical style for the centre of a dining-table.

STYLE

The greatest success in table decoration is achieved when all the components of a laid table have similar qualities, but how easy is it to recognize this? Fine bone china, sparkling silver and glass in traditional patterns will look well on highly polished tables, lace, damask or fine cloths, whereas sturdy oven-to-table ware, handthrown pottery, wooden handled cutlery and smoky Scandinavian glass will fit in better with a coarse linen cloth, rush mats or melamine place mats. These are obvious associations and it is very likely that if your taste in china is traditional then your cutlery and linen are also traditional, whereas those with a more 'modern' taste will have chosen bolder, texturally interesting tableware, linen and baskets.

A simple *pot-et-fleur* makes a long-lasting decoration for the family table. Four growing plants have three cut flowers added in a small container sunk into the compost

The same polished pine table gets a bolder treatment to complement the dark brown modern pottery and woven grass mats

SUITABILITY FOR THE OCCASION

There is also the purpose of the occasion to be considered. Is your table set for a formal celebration dinner party or a simple two-course family lunch? Is it for wine and cheese for 20 or an engagement party for 12, a romantic tête-a-tête dinner or a Bonfire Night sausage and mash affair for hungry children? Obviously the same kind of table will not be set for all of these, nor will the flowers be the same.

For the first occasion you would probably want to bring out all the best glass, silver and china and for the last, plastic beakers and disposable plates and cutlery. Even for this last event a decoration can be fun, but it will hardly be roses in a silver epergne; it is more likely to be piles of fruit in basketware or apple-headed, hessian-dressed 'guys' on sticks to provide the fruit course for the young guests. Even quite young party-goers can appreciate care with their party table and will enjoy finding that Linda has a red plate and mug with a red balloon marking her chair whereas Johnnie has green things and Sarah's are yellow.

COLOUR

This brings us to the question of colour which is dealt with more fully in Chapter 5 on page 59. After style and suitability for the occasion, colour is the feature which is likely to make the greatest impact – it makes an effective link between the various items on the table. If the colour of the cloth or place mats

Yellow place mats with lime-green candles and napkins complement the freshness of the blue and white china. In the centre of the candelabra a candlecup is fitted to hold an arrangement of yellow-centred white spray chrysanthemums and lime-green hellebores. Small blue hyacinths and grape hyacinths pick up the blue of the china

Many tones of brown from cream to nearly black are used for this supper table with strong textural interest. All the plant material is either dried or preserved with glycerine. The candles and napkins are rust-coloured.

32

echoes one or more of the colours in the china, or if candles and napkins do the same, then the table will have an integrated, well thought-out look and be well on the way to success. If the flower arrangement too, whether traditional or freestyle, also picks up one or more of these colours then the whole will knit together well.

A word of caution, though, about the careful matching of colours. All too often it is overdone: for example, yellow daffodils, tulips and forsythia are chosen to match a yellow cloth with yellow napkins and yellow candles. If all the yellows match, the effect will be flat and uninteresting. When choosing the flowers, range the yellows through from cream to nearly orange to give variety and interest and you will be far better pleased with the result.

Practical Guidelines for Success

HEIGHT

All writers on table decorations, in Victorian times and later, agree that flowers on the table must either be above or below the line of vision of the seated guests, so that conversation is not impeded. This rule was not always observed at large formal banquets where one was expected to converse primarily with those seated on the left and right. A picture of a banquet at The White House in 1899 shows a hedge of greenery and plants down the centre of the table over or through which conversation would have been quite impossible.

The greater informality evident today even at grand occasions, and certainly our more casual approach in the home, makes it essential that any table flowers are well below or lifted well above the eye-line. This means a maximum height of little over 30cm (1 foot) for a low arrangement or starting above 60cm (2 feet) for one raised in a tall container or on more than one level. It is not important if candles or one or two trails of fern or greenery come within the sight line, but even these should be fairly slender and compact. There is nothing more infuriating than having to dodge the greenery to make conversational small talk, and it becomes quite exasperating if the talk has taken a more serious turn. The likely result, at least at a private occasion, is that the host will simply remove the whole painstakingly contrived decoration and set it aside!

Today it is fairly rare to see raised arrangements for a seated meal except at larger formal occasions. Most table flowers are kept low and often in containers almost completely hidden by flowers and foliage. This does give a flat look to the table so candlesticks and candelabra are frequently used to provide vertical lines.

Buffet tables are different. Here people stand at the table to serve themselves and then move away (see page 47).

SIZE

I have seen various suggestions made about the proportion of the table area that may be allowed for the 'decorative unit' as it is sometimes called, varying from

33

2ft ---------▸

1ft -------▸

A reasonably clear space must be left for diners to converse across the table

one-third to one-sixth. This may well be appropriate for show or exhibition work but in my own experience, even one-sixth is too large for a practical table in a modern home. In these servant-less days, serving dishes and other items usually have to be placed on the table itself and a flower arrangement taking up one-sixth of the surface would soon be the worse for being knocked about, apart from the inconvenience of its dipping in the gravy and getting tangled up with the serving spoons.

Common sense must be the guide. Consider the size of the table and the number of place-settings required, then think of all the other bits and pieces that are nowadays usually set on the table – condiments, sauces, pickles, butter, bread basket, servers etc. *Then* decide how much space there is for a decoration and plan accordingly.

SHAPE AND PLACEMENT

Whilst it is often a sound idea to let the shape of the arrangement follow that of the table – round on round or square tables and long on narrow, oval or rectangular tables – do not let this be too inhibiting and consider something different from time to time.

Much will depend on the number of place-settings needed. If three are to sit at a square table then the fourth side might be used for the decoration, or with a rectangular table against a wall, the arrangement can be on that side, which has

34

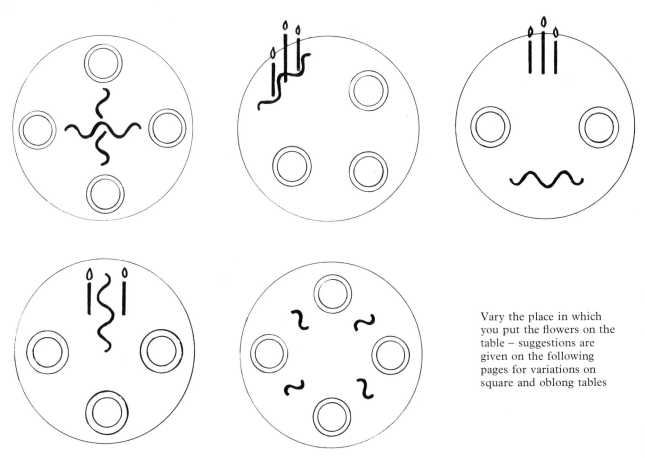

Vary the place in which you put the flowers on the table – suggestions are given on the following pages for variations on square and oblong tables

the added advantage that it will be viewed from three sides only. Candles, used with the flowers as part of the decoration of a table, can be placed in a variety of ways – but not at lunch time; leave candles for evening meals.

CONTAINERS

If the container is not going to show, any low dish or painted tin will suffice, but remember that table arrangements are seen at very close quarters and a nondescript container should be well hidden or camouflaged. Even if only a little is to show then be sure that it is either quite neutral or fits in with the table china and appointments. If the container is to be a feature of the decoration then it is often a good idea to use a piece from the service. At least be sure that it has the same quality as the rest of the table appointments.

A raised container may be a candelabra or single candlestick, a cherub or figurine holding a cup aloft, a dessert tazza, compote or footed dish, and this is usually a feature in its own right. Here again, bear in mind the suitability of the piece to the rest of the table and the occasion. A gilt cherub can look quite out of place with unglazed ovenware and a sturdy brass or pewter candlestick equally so with fine silver and delicate china.

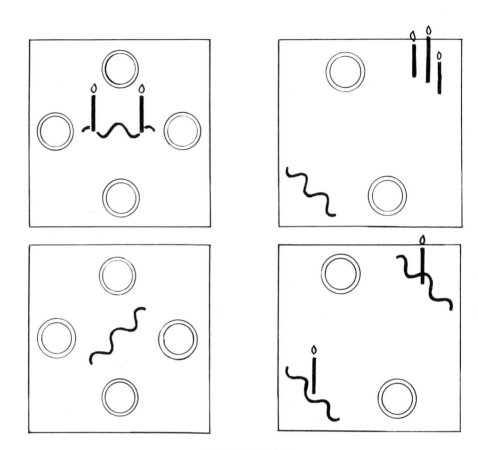

MECHANICS

Keep these firm and unobtrusive. Water-retaining foam is very suitable for use on tables as it does away with the need for water in the container which can be knocked and spilled, marking the polished table or cloth. For an arrangement on an average modern dining-table a small round of *Oasis* foam, held in place on a pronged holder secured to the container with putty-type adhesive, should be quite adequate for a massed style arrangement. Whatever is chosen, make sure it cannot be seen even close to. Choose the smallest piece of foam that will be adequate. Larger pieces are more difficult to cover. Rusty pinholders, spiky pieces of wire-netting or uncovered *Oasis* are not attractive to look at and quickly detract from the flowers.

PLANT MATERIALS

Except, perhaps, for a specimen flower or small arrangement on a desk, no flower decoration is seen at closer quarters than the one on a meal table. Guests may be seated within a foot of it, so above all, it is important that it should be clean. Foliage must be well washed and conditioned and all blemished leaves and petals removed. No one wants earwigs or greenfly crawling near their food.

It has been argued that strongly scented flowers such as hyacinths and

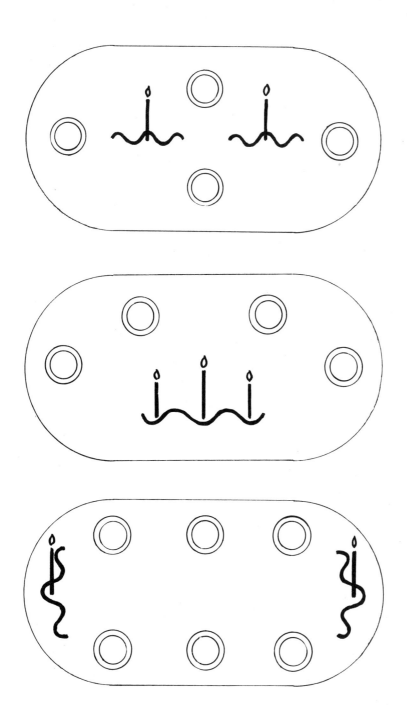

A basket makes a suitable container for spring flowers on a table with boldly patterned Swedish table mats

pungent herbs like rosemary or rue should not be used in arrangements near food because of possible conflict with the smell and taste of the food itself and also because heavy scents are objectionable to some people. There is reason in this. I love the smell of hyacinths but many people dislike it and even I wonder if the heavy scent goes well with fish or onion dishes.

Since one of the assets of a table decoration is that it can provide a talking point at meals, different and unusual plant material will excite comment. People take roses for granted, but are often surprised by the use of rose hips. The black berries of tree ivy are almost always remarked on and yellow-berried holly, as opposed to the more usual red, invariably attracts interest. Hosta leaves are well-known, but the flower spikes far less so; the silky seedheads of old man's beard or travellers' joy (*Clematis vitalba*), the leaf-stripped sprays of lime tree flowers or those of laurustinus (*Viburnum tinus*) are less often recognized than one might expect. The simple question 'What are these flowers?' can trigger off general conversation in the moment or two when everyone settles down and before the first course begins.

The old idea that only certain flowers like roses, carnations and sweet peas

An effective Victorian-style centre-piece uses a container home-made from a length of dowelling and empty steak-pie tins covered with silver doilies. Set on a mirror base it combines fruit, foliage and flowers for a winter table. (*Arranger: Joan Dyson. Photo: The Flower Arranger*)

It is never easy to put flowers with a strongly patterned fabric. This formal cone is effective because it uses yellow-centred white daisies repeating those on the cloth

should be used on the table has long since been discarded, but even so, people tend still to be very conventional, believing that only florist's flowers or the 'best' flowers from the garden should be used. The main criteria, however, should be suitability of colour and form, attractiveness and interest.

USING A BASE

A base underneath an arrangement can help to protect the table or cloth from spills, but it can also lift the flowers, however little, into greater prominence; add colour to enhance the flowers; unite flowers and candles or flowers with an accessory; link the arrangement and its colours more closely with china, place mats or napkins. It is quite surprising how the colour of a base will gleam

40

A stylized 'tree' of white daisies in a white-painted flower-pot on a garden table
stands out because of its strong geometric shape

through the arrangement, especially if there is an overhead light, so adding
depth and interest. Raising the arrangement also creates a little more space for
serving dishes and spoons.

HOW MUCH PLANT MATERIAL?

Beginners often need a guide to how many flowers they will need to pick or buy. So much, of course, depends on the size of the arrangement and what other plant material is available in the way of foliage, berries or seedheads. But, for the long, low arrangement that is popular today on the average dining table, it is perfectly possible to make an arrangement with foliage and just one stem of, say, spray chrysanthemums, carefully cut for maximum effect. It is not easy,

Branches of apple-blossom with two tulips in a low bowl have an oriental look and would be effective for a meal serving Chinese dishes – even a Chinese 'take-away' tastes better when attractively set out

nor will it be very colourful. With two sprays, if they are long heads and not bunchy at the top, then you can do quite well. This means about ten or twelve flowers, including buds, provided foliage is available. If you have, or can afford, twice as many, then the whole thing becomes much easier and much more colourful.

When picking or buying, try to have two different *shapes* of flowers, one round (e.g. rose, daisy-type, dahlia, carnation, daffodil) and one in a spike or spray (e.g. freesia, stock, larkspur). The same applies to foliage. Three different shapes are desirable – tapering sprays or long leaves, bushier fillers and larger, rounder leaves or rosettes of leaves for the centre.

Artistic Guidelines

It is one thing to give practical guidelines about size and height or mechanics, but it is much more difficult to advise on what I have rather grandly called the artistic aspect, that is, on deciding what to use and how to use it. Students come to classes and say: 'But I don't know what flowers to use or buy' and then having bought some, deplore that: 'Whatever I do I seem to end up with a shapeless, muddly arrangement.'

DECIDING WHAT TO USE

My first question to the student is: 'What have you already got?' We discuss what the table is like, what wood it is made of, what cloths or place mats are possible, and most important of all, what the china is like. If it is neutral then almost anything goes, and that, in itself, may not be much help. But if it has colour and/or a pattern then something in these will give a lead. It is not necessary to go for the obvious; it may be a good idea to pick up the second most important colour if there is more than one, and consider whether the result would be effective with flowers and, say, napkins, repeating it. If the china or linen has a flower or leaf pattern, is it possible to use the real flower or leaf in the arrangement? Or something similar in colour and shape? Are there any associations with the pattern? 'Willow pattern' for instance, suggests using willow, iris and water plants, or an oriental-style arrangement, and a geometric pattern may suggest cut and clipped stems and leaves for the outline framework of the flowers and simple round shapes like daisies.

What food will be served? There may be an idea here. Seafood can be complemented with an arrangement in a shell, using plant material that evokes the sea, such as succulents, grey leaves, blue thistle-type flowers and perhaps dried seaweed curls; a Chinese meal can have an oriental low bowl of blossom and a few flowers; goulash flavoured with paprika could use red and green peppers in the table decoration. The possibilities are many. So next time you seek inspiration for a table arrangement, think about:

The *colour* on the china or linen
The *pattern* on the china or linen
The *food* to be served
The *occasion*.

In late autumn, evergreen leaves and berries with flowers from the florist can be used to reflect the colours of the cups set for after-dinner coffee. (*Photo: Jeremy Hall*)

44

SETTING ABOUT THE ARRANGEMENT

Let's assume that to start with you plan a simple, low arrangement for the centre of a table, so that it will be seen from all sides. The container will not be important as it will show very little, so a small, low dish is ideal, with a round of *Oasis* held in place on a pronged plastic holder. You have some flowers and leaves and are ready to start. At the risk of sounding like 'arranging by numbers', I suggest the following plan as a sound one to follow:

1   If possible work on the table where the arrangement will be. Cover the centre with plastic sheeting to protect the table while you work.
2   Establish an outline to the size you want. Using tapering sprays of leaves or small flowers or buds for preference, fix the framework for your design – the length, width and height. If you are using candles in the arrangement put them in now (see page 69). These are the 'bones' of the design.

If you need to have a round arrangement for a round or square table, put in *three* outline stems, dividing the circle into thirds, rather than quarters (see diagram) which helps to avoid it becoming too crowded.

The outline for a long, low arrangement

A bird's eye view of the outline for a round arrangement

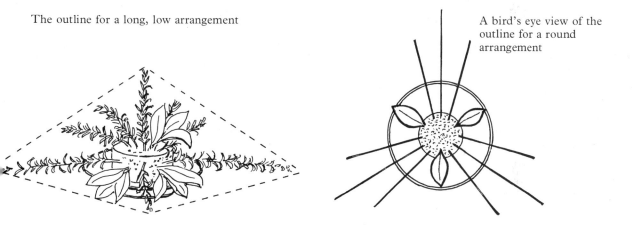

3   Add one or two stems, either leaf or flower, a little shorter than the first, following the lines already set. Don't have any stems longer than the 'bones'. Keep turning the arrangement as you work so that all sides get equal attention.
4   Before going any further, use some larger leaves or bushier plant material to help obscure the block of foam. Try to avoid a frill round the block and have some leaves vertical to help marry the tallest stems with the length and width.
5   The largest flowers should be kept till last. These will be the shortest stems, concentrating the colour near the centre. Again, try to avoid a frill, varying the stem lengths, tilting some flowers up, some down and some to show their profile.
6   Now sit down if you've been standing, or vice versa, to see your work from a new angle. Where there are obvious gaps add a flower or leaf, but restrain

yourself from trying to fill every hole. Each flower needs to have space around it and it is quite unnecessary to cover up every tiny piece of *Oasis* that you can see. As long as a leaf or flower or stem breaks up the visual line, that is enough.

7   Add water if needed, spray the arrangement gently with water, remove the plastic and the table is ready to be laid.

TOTAL HARMONY

The successful table and its decoration will be one where a link of overall style runs through everything. Sometimes there is a discordant note. A colour, perhaps, a line? If you can identify it then take it away or make an alteration; you will never feel happy about it otherwise. Sometimes the wrong touch is harder to be sure about and it is no more than a nagging suspicion that somehow you could have done better. Try to discover what went wrong, because you learn so much from a recognized mistake. But there is always another table and another arrangement to be done, and when the design does all harmonize, the satisfaction is great.

CHAPTER 4

Special Occasion Tables

Nature not only places abundantly at our disposal the flowers with which to carry out our schemes, but she surrounds and stimulates us with endless suggestions, which we should ever patiently study and faithfully follow; she will then never fail to solve every problem with which we may find ourselves confronted.
R.F. FELTON, *British Floral Decoration,* 1910

Buffet Tables

oday's hostess, faced with a small dining-room and lack of domestic help to prepare and wait at table, frequently resorts to a buffet meal when entertaining more than six to eight people. The food is laid out for guests to serve themselves, or perhaps to be served with some part of the meal by the host or hostess. They then take their plates away and usually sit at smaller tables in the same, or adjoining rooms, on the stairs, on the floor or wherever there is space. The main serving table is the focus of attention. Guests will be standing by it or moving round it, so two things are especially important for the flowers: height and stability.

Low, spreading decorations will hardly be seen and anyway they interfere with the serving. A tall or raised container not only lifts the flowers out of the way of the food, but it also has far greater impact, since it will be virtually at eye-level. Aim at an arrangement which is bold and striking.

Stability is also essential if catastrophes are to be avoided. The flowers must certainly not be top-heavy. There is a great deal of movement around a buffet table and a certain amount of jostling is inevitable, but provided you keep in mind where the guests will be, it is not difficult to decide where to place the decorations.

Candelabra holding both candles and flowers in candle-cups are popular; tall vases, provided they are sturdy and well weighted at the base (part-filled with sand if necessary) can be used effectively; wrought iron and wooden stands, or other purpose-made constructions of driftwood and stripped tree ivy used as a support for one or more arrangements, are very decorative. It is often possible to stand a container on a small table, saucepan stand, set of shelves, bamboo stool or pile of baskets to give the necessary height. If the buffet table is against a wall, consider an arrangement fixed on the wall, or garlands looped across it.

Left A garden statue makes an interesting group with just foliage and fruit for a wine and cheese buffet supper
Right Tiered baskets make a 76 cm (30 in.) high tower for autumn buffet flowers

One eye-catching idea is to suspend from the ceiling, over the table, tiers of containers in macramé hangers, or, equally effective, is a simple construction of three cardboard circles or round cake-boards in diminishing sizes threaded onto cords, knotted to prevent each layer slipping out of place. With a light-weight container on each arrange pretty flowers and trailing foliage in a cascade (see diagram).

GARLANDS AND SWAGS

Garlands and swags across the skirting of a buffet table look most attractive – provided people are not standing in front of it! By the time several guests have moved in to serve themselves, nothing of the garlanding will be seen. So consider carefully how much will be visible and for how long, before you decide to take the extra time and trouble to make garlands. A quicker and less expensive alternative is shown on the wedding table in the colour section. Tinted sheets cover the table which is swagged with inexpensive butter muslin

Bright magenta and lime green bring a touch of sophistication to a dinner party for four

Romantic cream and white with lace-edged mats recall the 1930s

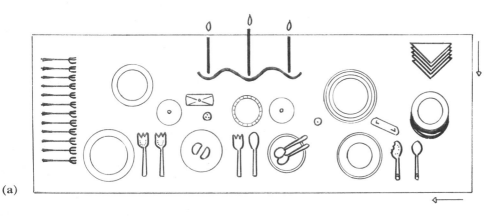

(a)

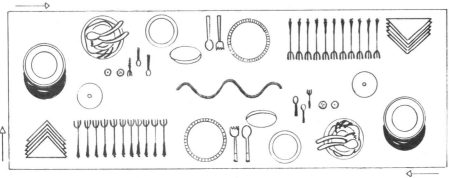

(b)

Planning the movement round a buffet table where it is (a) next to a wall and (b) out in the open with two main serving areas. Place the flowers where they will be out of the way

and a small posy pinned to each apex. The posies were arranged in half a round of polythene-wrapped *Oasis* taped, to protect the cloth, into a small plastic food tray from a supermarket. A loop of wire through the top enabled it to be pinned in place easily. Curling ribbons added to the festive look.

It is usually worth considering swags for the bridal cake table or the top table at a wedding as everyone will be looking towards these during the speeches and toasts.

SMALL INDIVIDUAL TABLES

To keep a planned, totally harmonious look, it is important that small tables should, in some way, have their decor linked to the main buffet table. If it is not possible to use exactly the same kind of flowers (and those on the large table may be too big) then repeat the colour, use some buds, a little of the same foliage and perhaps the same ribbons, or a candle of the same colour for an evening party. The colour of the cloths and napkins can provide an additional link with the main table.

A tiered decoration to hang over a buffet table out of the way of the food and the guests

49

For this marquee wedding reception the flowers are all in pink and white and arrangements for small tables on the lawn stand ready to be put outside before the guests arrive. (*Arranger: Janet Wesley*)

Weddings

Wedding flowers are not always white, but they do tend to be pastel in colouring and to include white to keep a light, romantic look. The colours of the bridesmaids' dresses are often picked up, sometimes in a paler tint to avoid heaviness. Today there are absolutely no rules or conventions about which flowers are suitable, but, for the most part, the style of arranging is still traditional with massed mixed flowers.

Variegated foliages are especially useful to achieve lightness and, usually, not too difficult to obtain. There are so many today available in Britain: ivies of many kinds, privet, pittosporum, cupressus, weigela, euonymus, hosta, pelargonium and holly, to name but a selection. Grey and silver leaves are useful too: artemisia, eucalyptus, senecio, whitebeam, cineraria, santolina and rue.

CUTTING THE COST

Wedding flowers certainly need not be expensive. There is a good deal available from gardens and hedgerows, provided, of course, that one cuts with care and restraint, and never too much from one tree or plant.

In early spring the silver pussy willows are lovely to use with bought spring flowers, or even on their own, tied with white and pastel ribbons. If the wedding is in April or May, there is blossom in white and pink, lilac (syringa) and in June or July there is mock orange blossom (philadelphus). In June the roadsides are lined with cow parsley or Queen Anne's lace, followed a little later by the similar, but taller, wild hemlock. In autumn old man's beard or travellers' joy with its silky seedheads in graceful trails and sprays (remove all the leaves) can be used as late as November.

50

Wedding Anniversaries

1st	Paper	13th	Lace
2nd	Cotton	14th	Ivory
3rd	Leather	15th	Crystal
4th	Fruit and flowers	20th	China
5th	Wood	25th	Silver
6th	Sugar or iron	30th	Pearl
7th	Wool or copper	35th	Coral
8th	Bronze or pottery	40th	Ruby
9th	Pottery or willow	50th	Gold
10th	Tin	55th	Emerald
11th	Steel	60th	Diamond
12th	Silk or linen		

Dried leaves and seedheads in a tall modern pot, dramatically lit by a ceiling spotlight, add interest to a wedding anniversary buffet table in a modern home. Even the gourds and fruits in the dish are dried, with a few plastic grapes

The popularly marked wedding anniversaries of silver, ruby and gold are well-known; the others are less well remembered and some of them less certainly named as the list shows. But there is inspiration here for the arranger of flowers for the table and an interesting challenge to match the decorations to the occasion.

The colours – ivory, silver (white and grey), pearl, coral, ruby, gold (yellow) and emerald should present no problems, but it is more effective to use not only flowers of the appropriate colour but foliage tinged with it and perhaps fruit which repeats the same hue. Even though the available china may not match, it is usually possible to provide some small colour link which makes the table look planned. It is never as difficult as it sounds if one is prepared to think about it in good time!

The metals – iron, copper, tin, bronze, steel, silver and gold – should not be difficult either, as least as far as the container is concerned. Now that metallic paints and sprays are so generally obtainable it is easy to spray a container and some dried plant material in the appropriate metallic finish. The secret of success, I think, is not to overdo this. Use some metallic-painted leaves and seedheads, for example, with fresh flowers and fresh, dried or glycerined foliage in similar tints and shades. The result will be far more attractive than a complete dried arrangement sprayed all one colour.

A little thought will suggest possibilities for other anniversaries: the use of brown glycerined foliage which has a leathery look, the felt-backed leaves of some rhododendrons and dried bulrushes looking like suede for the third; driftwood, bark and branches for the fifth; wild cow parsley or lace-cap hydrangeas for the thirteenth; pussy willows and woven baskets for the ninth; cut glass and white flowers for the fifteenth and sixtieth. Don't forget the possibility of underlining the name of the occasion by using bases or accessories linked with the title.

Birthdays

Flowers for a birthday party, whether a buffet or sit-down meal, can be much more personal. At this type of party, the flowers are to please one person in particular and can do so by using a favourite colour; by trying to interpret his or her personality as amusing, romantic, sporty, musical or sophisticated; or emphasizing a special hobby or interest such as tennis, travelling, disco dancing or the ballet. There is more scope for this in an arrangement for a buffet table, but it is still possible to arrange a very apt centre-piece for a seated occasion, without overdoing the accessories or taking up too much table space. Emphasize the personal aspect and it will be appreciated by everyone.

Christmas

The traditional Christmas colours are the green, red and white of evergreen leaves, holly berries and snow. To these, gold and silver have been added, possibly because of the shine and semblance of sunshine they bring to cold

Hardly table 'flowers' but of greater interest to a small boy for his birthday! The moonscape rocket is made from two half-pint cream cartons with paper nose cone and cardboard gantry. Trees are made from liquorice sweets threaded on wooden skewers. The base is a ceiling tile landscaped with broken lumps from polystyrene packing

A Christmas supper table set with scarlet centre runner, napkins and candles. The flowers are red roses and single white spray chrysanthemums arranged with holly and artificial berries. In the background is a wreath of evergreens with artificial Christmas roses and fruits

northern mid-winters. Today it is possible, with flowers of paper, plastic, ribbon, fabric and those grown in greenhouses, to have many different colours.

For Christmas table decorations then, it is a question of deciding whether to have evergreens and fresh flowers; painted and glittered dried and preserved plant materials; frankly artificial plastic foliage and silk or homemade flowers, or a combination of all three to suit one's decor and purse.

Even the traditionalists, as a rule, are not averse to the added gleam of gold paint and the effective gold, silver, copper and mother-of-pearl finishes that can be achieved with today's plastics. Ribbons and baubles add their own touch of gaiety. Decorative candles come into their own and gilt angels, cherubs and bells are accepted as accessories for the flowers.

Left Candles and gilt plastic sprays on a patterned cloth for Christmas
Right A wholly artificial arrangement is acceptable at Christmas or on New Year's
Eve and makes a striking buffet decoration

FLOWERS AND FOLIAGE

In Britain, holly and ivy are the most important foliages, and the variegated
varieties much sought after to bring lightness to the heavier dark greens.
Aucuba and eleagnus with their splashes of gold are equally welcome.
Cupressus, yew, pine, laurustinus, rosemary, choisya, bay, skimmia and
rosemary are all available at Christmas time and invaluable for garlands,
wreaths and other arrangements. If it is not a good year for berries then
artificial ones are usually available and worth wiring in clusters to twist in with
the leaves.

Red flowers available at the florist's include single and spray carnations,
anemones, and sometimes gladioli and roses; for white there are single and
spray chrysanthemums and carnations, chincherinchees and lilies. House
plants include poinsettia, cyclamen and azalea in red and white or cream.

55

FRUIT

Fruit is colourful and decorative, and has an added advantage of being edible when the decoration has served its purpose. Use it with foliage to provide round shapes instead of flowers; add it to arrangements of flowers and leaves to give added richness, or arrange it casually or in a pyramid, with just a few evergreen leaves to decorate the dish or stand.

The Christmas table decorations in Colonial Williamsburg, USA make excellent use of evergreens and colourful fruit and similar arrangements are made in other American homes. They use to great effect the contrast between the dark, glossy green of magnolia, holly, laurel and boxwood leaves, and the softer pine, spruce, rosemary and cedar with brilliant red apples, lemons, oranges, cones, berries and grapes.

Italians, too, often use fruit piled on a dish or arranged in a basket as a table centrepiece, and include richly coloured peppers, tomatoes and aubergines. Belgian arrangers will include sweet corn, cauliflowers, artichokes and kale among their flowers for greater impact. In Britain this combination of foliage,

Breakfast at Easter-time calls for a simple, uncontrived arrangement

fruit and vegetables is not used often enough, which is surprising when there are home-grown apples and pears available all the winter, as well as cones and nuts.

Another attractive custom from Williamsburg is wreathing important serving dishes and bowls, or laying fruit and sprigs of greenery along colourful ribbons laid in a cross shape in the centre of the table.

Easter

Easter colours are gold, yellow and white. The arum lily which graces church altars at Easter is generally too large for the average table arrangement, but forsythia, daffodils, narcissi, tulips and primroses all lend their golden colour to a time of rejoicing.

Mixed colours, too, are the very essence of spring and a shallow basket with a handle holding a mixture of anemones, hellebores, hyacinths, polyanthus and grape hyacinths will always look effective, especially if colourful foil-wrapped Easter eggs are being placed on the table as gifts. Rabbits, fluffy yellow chickens, bird's nests with confectionery eggs can all be used as accessories. Children as well as adults enjoy a moss garden. Using a round or oblong tray or shallow dish that will fit the centre of the table, pack the surface with moss. Add a stone or two to vary the height and tuck in little bunches of small flowers and leaves to create a garden of colourful clumps rather like those shown in the 'millefleurs' tapestries of the Middle Ages.

For a christening tea pastel-coloured flowers are combined with two cherubs. These 'china' figurines are really cheap brown plastic candle-holders painted with white gloss paint and filled with a mixture of tiny real and silk flowers and sprigs of greenery

Christenings

Even though today young mothers dress their new babies in brilliant colours and even brown and navy blue, christenings are still fairly traditional affairs with flowers for the table arranged in mixed pastel colours or 'blue for a boy, pink for a girl'. The cradle and bootee type containers available at many florists are really quite difficult to arrange attractively, and it is probably more effective to use an ordinary white, silver or pastel-coloured container and let the colours and pretty, simple flowers be the focus of attention. Inexpensive plastic and plaster cherubs and *amorini* are widely obtainable and these make very apt accessories and decorations for the christening table.

Other Special Events

Hallowe'en and Guy Fawkes' Night both lend themselves to interpretative decorations and it can be fun to carry the theme, however simply, into the table flowers. The fluffy seedheads of rosebay willowherb or the wild or garden clematis can suggest smoke, and the brilliant reds, oranges and yellows of autumnal dahlias, chrysanthemums, red hot pokers, Chinese lanterns and many berries will evoke fire and fireworks. Masks, broomsticks, black cats, witches and guys can easily be made or cut from paper to be used as accessories. Nightlights in hollowed-out pumpkins, mangel-wurzels or swedes, or in perforated empty tins, cast an eerie, decorative light. The Hallowe'en custom of 'bobbing apples' indicates that apples can figure largely in any decoration.

Each and every occasion has some quality or special aspect which can help the arranger of the table flowers. Look it up in the dictionary, encyclopaedia or thesaurus; the definition or explanation may contain an idea for an arrangement. Do a little homework on the occasion, whatever it is, and you are more likely to achieve a good result.

A large piece of driftwood and seashore finds with garden foliage, seedheads and berries made a talking point for a fish-and-chip supper

58

CHAPTER 5

Colour and Lighting

Colour is king. Colour in flowers is the greatest quality of all. Colour is the attractive force, for colourless flowers would be as meaningless as straw. . . .
W. CLEAVER HARRY, *The Manual of Floral Designing*, 1923

e live today in a colour-conscious world. It is difficult to recall the days when sheets and towels, tablecloths and napkins were white; and so were underwear, toilet paper, babyclothes and tennis kit; when telephones were all black and Henry Ford said that a customer could have a car any colour he liked as long as it was black. Since World War II and the coming of colour in films, television and magazines, everything is in brilliant technicolour.

Today it is possible to have colourful china and linen on tables and to mix and match even quite subtle hues to make exciting colour combinations. With a little care and forethought we can all have attractive tables with colour-linked flower arrangements. Knowing how to use colour to good effect is far more important than buying expensive flowers.

Learning about Colour

There are those who have an 'eye for colour' or an instinctive colour sense. Since colour is probably the greatest single factor in effective table decoration, those who feel they lack this inherent flair do have to work just a little harder to understand colour and how it works.

The theory is not difficult. It has been repeated in book after book on flower arrangement. The readers who understand simply skip it and those who do not understand tend to skip it anyway as boring, academic detail they can do without. But if colour *is* so important in all forms of flower arrangement, and especially in table decorations where flowers, china, linen, cutlery and glass are to achieve a harmonious whole, then it is worth making the effort to understand it.

Everyone knows the rainbow colours: red, orange, yellow, green, blue, indigo and violet and many children learned the mnemonic to help remember the order: 'Richard of York Gained Battles in Vain' (ROYGBIV). Most people remember that red and yellow have to be mixed to make orange, yellow and blue to make green, and blue and red to produce violet. So red, yellow and blue are the *primary* colours or *hues* from which all others can be made, and orange, green and violet are *secondary*. Mix each of these with its neighbouring colour and you have the *tertiary* colours.

To each of these primary, secondary and tertiary hues black, white and grey (itself a mixture of black and white) may be added. This will give *shades* (black added), *tints* (white added) and *tones* (grey added).

The Colour Wheel or Circle

From this artists devised the colour wheel. It is a convention, of course, but a useful one since it provides a basis on which to develop and explain colour theory. The main difficulty with colour wheels, however, is that they tend to suggest that there is a firm dividing line between each hue and the next. But

A colour wheel with the names commonly used

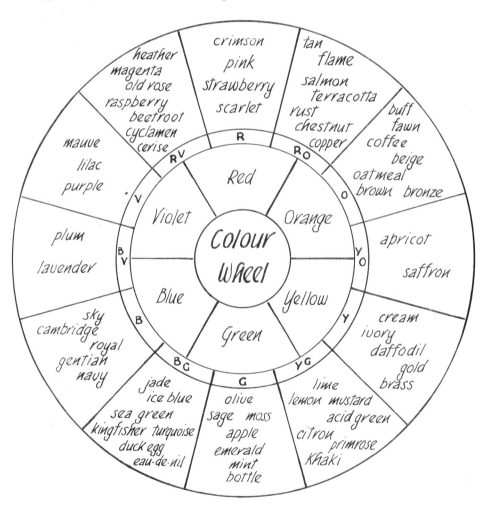

60

who can say when red actually becomes red-orange, and where exactly red-orange merges into orange-yellow? For the flower arranger there is the added consideration that few flowers are exactly all one colour since petals are often shaded, streaked and mottled. So mathematical precision is not what is required so much as a general understanding of the way colour works. But colour wheels do have a use in that when we try to match or describe a colour they help us to analyse it more closely and carefully. We have to reason out that 'it's a very yellow orange' or that 'the pink has a lot of blue in it'.

This chart on page 60 shows colours by their familiar names, fitted into a colour wheel. Since our perception of, and reaction to, colour is very personal and subjective, this can only be a guide. What I call 'duck-egg blue' you may call 'turquoise', but we both mean a mixture of green and blue with some white added. While no amount of hard work will ever replace a natural eye for colour, a conscious awareness of colour and a willingness to experiment with it will sharpen one's reactions.

Colour Exercises

If you feel you are not good with colour, try these exercises:

1 Examine a flower closely. Identify *out loud* all the colours, tints and shades you can see in it – include the stamens, reverse side of the petals, the colour deep down in the throat, the stem and the calyx cupping the flower. Try to be exact. If it is pink, it is an orangey-pink or a mauve-pink? Are the stamens really black or a very dark brown, or blue, or purple?

2 Acquire a full set of paint colour cards from a do-it-yourself shop and try a matching test: pick out the colour on the card nearest to something you are wearing, the wallpaper, a book cover, curtains, kitchen plastic bowl, pot lids, anything. Just exercise your ability to recognize exact colours.

3 With the colour cards in your hand *mentally* match the colour to something you know well (a jersey, a cushion, a pot plant flower, bathroom towel, car, lipstick) *but cannot see*, so that you have to remember the colour. Find out how accurate you were; if you're weak on greens, for example, practise more on them.

Any game of this sort improves colour and tone awareness and helps to train the eye. Consequently, everything – anything – becomes much more interesting to look at.

Working Out Colour Schemes

This is where the colour wheel can be very useful.

MONOCHROMATIC SCHEMES

Mono = one, chroma = colour; so a monochromatic scheme means a group of tints, tones and shades all based on *one* main colour e.g. pink, bright red and maroon based on red, or cream, yellow and gold based on yellow. Such colour schemes are attractive and easy to use. One can hardly go wrong.

ANALOGOUS OR ADJACENT COLOURS

Any two or three colours with all their tints, tones and shades, lying next to each other in the colour wheel, are called analogous. They will all have the same primary or secondary hue in their make-up, however much that parent colour has been modified. For example, it is easy to see that red, red-orange and orange are analogous or blue violet, violet and violet red; but it is not always quite so easy to appreciate that in the two groups mentioned here one can also have, say, crimson, peach and bronze or lavender, purple, beetroot and old rose. Because these groups of analogous colours do have this common parent as a link, they are easy to use together and fairly 'safe' because in whatever amounts, tints or shades you use them an overall harmony will prevail.

COMPLEMENTARY OR CONTRASTING COLOUR SCHEMES

Colours which lie opposite (or almost opposite) each other on the colour wheel are known as complementary. So red is complementary to green, green-blue to red-orange and so on. These complementary pairs are often called contrasting, and colour schemes using two complementaries are much more vivid than analogous groups and consequently more difficult to handle. Nevertheless, they are exciting, have impact and are well worth experimenting with to get the right balance. Generally, it is better to use far more of one colour than the other. The second colour becomes an accent rather than an equal partner.

Another useful tip when using complementaries is to avoid using the same purity of colour for each. Pure red and pure green are difficult to put together, as both are strong and vivid and they tend to cancel each other out. So either use a lot of red with one or two touches of green or use tints and shades together such as pink with bottle-green or crimson with sage green. Other complementary pairs worth considering are:

clover – acid yellow	tan – ice-blue
mulberry – primrose	duck-egg – vermilion
lilac – old gold	navy – beige
coffee – Cambridge blue	orange – navy.

To translate these schemes into ideas for table decorations, perhaps based on your china, is not difficult, as in the chart on the next page.

Obviously the chart can only give examples; the possibilities of subtle variations in mixing, matching and contrasting are almost endless. Use the chart and the wheel, remembering the colours you already have in the way of china, linen and accessories, and work out a few theoretical colour schemes. Then match them up with flowers, leaves and fruits in the garden, or at the florist's or fruiterer's or in your store cupboard of dried, preserved and artificial materials. You will be quite surprised at the possibilities already there, or at least quite easy to obtain.

China	Colour Scheme*	Linen	Flower arrangement	Candles/ accessories
Dark blue or blue/white e.g. 'Willow Pattern'	M	Blue	Flowers in many tints and shades of blue, with blue-grey foliage	Blue or white
	A	Mauve, turquoise	Mauve and purple flowers, blue-green foliage	Mauve or turquoise
	C	Pale apricot, beige, or burnt orange	Brilliant orange flowers, touches of apricot	Orange
Pink or pink/white patterned e.g. roses on white ground	M	Deeper or lighter pink cloth – napkins to tone but not match	Light and darker pinks, reddish or grey foliage. White if in china	Pink to maroon matching one pink used or white
	A	Mauve or salmon pink	Pinks ranging from mauve to salmon, all tones	Mauve or salmon pink
	C	Dark or medium green, or lime	Greens and some flowers matching the pink of the china	Dark green or lime
Oatmeal or beige, plain or with darker brown decoration	M	Dark brown, rust	Dried and glycerined leaves, dried seedheads, rust flowers	Brown or tan
	A	Apricot, yellow or flame	Yellow and orange flowers, brown and yellow foliages	Yellow or orange
	C	Pale turquoise or sky blue	Various blues with blue-greens and some tan foliage	Turquoise
Plain pale green or white and green patterned	M	Soft lime-green, deeper green napkins	Foliages in mixed greens – with green flowers, buds or berries	Lime green
	A	Primrose yellow cloth with deep yellow napkins	Yellow, white and green	Yellow
	C	Bright pink or maroon	Flowers in pink and red tones	Pink or darkish red

*M = monochromatic
A = analogous
C = complementary

Colour at Night

In the dark there is no colour; black takes over, lightened by areas of grey. In the dwindling light of evening, colours begin to become greyed, until they are no more than areas of varying greys. But I am sure you will have noticed how, in the garden, the white flowers stand out, becoming almost fluorescent for a brief while before they too fade into the greyness. White is said to have a high 'luminosity', that is, it shows up well in poor light.

Taking the principal colours in order, the next most luminous is yellow, followed by orange, then red and green which are roughly equal, then blue and finally violet. These are pure colours, not modified by any mixing with black or white into a tint, a tone or a shade. It is easy to see, however, that a *tint* of any of the colours will have greater luminosity by reason of the addition of white. Similarly, a *shade* of any colour will be less luminous, and the darker the shade the nearer to black and 'no-colour' it will be, especially when seen in poor light. From this it becomes obvious that the darker shades, many blues and most violets are better avoided for evening meal tables. So many of these non-luminous colours end up looking black and in a table decoration that can mean that the dark green leaves, gorgeous dark red roses, deep blue delphiniums or purple campanula that looked so well in good daylight will simply look like black holes in an arrangement later in the day.

For evening a much safer choice is cream, pale pink, apricot, peach, buff, lime and yellow.

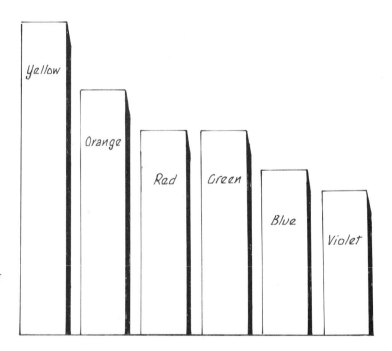

The relative luminosity of the principal colours, showing that yellow is more easily seen than violet in a poor light

64

How Lighting Affects Colours

For evening meals, except perhaps in high summer, we have to use some form of artificial lighting, and each different type affects colours in a different way. Generally, the 'luminosity' scale holds good, but some colours are changed by the light in which they are seen.

ELECTRIC LIGHT

Most household lighting today in living rooms is electric tungsten (the usual pear-shaped 'bulb') which gives a much yellower light than daylight. (Towards dusk, turn on a light indoors then look out of the window; the daylight outside will look surprisingly blue.) On the dining table tungsten light will enhance yellows, oranges and reds, but will deaden most blues and purples.

Fluorescent strip lighting, which many of us have in kitchens or above window pelmets or under shelving has the opposite effect. It tends to enhance blues and purples, giving them a vibrant look. Reds, however, are generally muddied into brown, and yellows tend to become neutralized.

CANDLELIGHT

Candles also give a yellowish light, but it is much dimmer than tungsten lighting. Candlelight is often chosen for the table because it is flattering to skin tones but for the same reason it will be unflattering to blues, purples and darker shades.

SHADOWS

While considering the type of lighting, it is useful also to consider the source and direction of the light. It is surprising what a difference this can make. If you have ever arranged flowers in the kitchen and then carried them into another room only to be disappointed with the result, it may well have been that the light was then coming from a window on the opposite side. The shadows will have been in a different place when you started and now the whole tone and balance of the colours in the arrangement will be altered. Whenever you can, arrange flowers *in situ*.

Overhead lighting will give brilliance to the top flowers and cast a pool of shadow beneath the arrangement. Lighting from one side only may cast half the arrangement into shadow. Low lights cast shadows upwards and may reveal some of the mechanics which would be better hidden! There is the charming story of the Victorian hostess of some standing who insisted that the servants renewed the candles when they were half burned down in the middle of dinner. When asked why this extravagance was considered necessary she replied that new candles shed a soft flattering glow on the diners' faces but when the candles burned down below the level of the faces all the wrinkles and double chins were accentuated! The same sort of thing can happen to the flowers.

As long as the flower arranger is aware of colour and shadow changes there is little real problem in choosing the best colours for the table for an evening meal. To avoid annoyance and disappointment, however, it does help to arrange the flowers in the lighting that will actually be used. It may seem a little odd to pull the curtains and light the candles on a brilliant summer afternoon, but it may, for a special occasion, be well worth it.

Candles

The present-day fashion of positioning 'pull-down' lights over the dining-table has focussed attention, perhaps as never before, on the table *centre*. The family or guests walking into a dining room or dining area will see first the spotlit table, its settings and its flowers. Since the centre is the most popular place for the flowers, they take the limelight. How gratifying for the arranger, but what a challenge at the same time!

However, in spite of the widespread availability of electric light, it is surprising how the popularity of candlelight for dining has endured. Nowadays, admittedly, it is usually augmented by subdued electric lights elsewhere in the room, but through all the technical advances in lighting from rush-nip lights, to oil-lamps, to gas and then electricity, the popularity of candles has hardly wavered.

There is no doubt that candles are the hostess's and flower arranger's favourite accessory. We no longer need the candles for light, though we may enjoy its flattery, but we use them for decoration.

Until the 1920s, candles were mostly cream or white in colour, though eighteenth-century colonial settlers in America discovered how to produce a green wax by boiling the berries of the bayberry tree, an indigenous species of myrtle. Vegetable dyes, however, were not colourfast, and candles coloured this way faded rapidly. It was also difficult to achieve good burning without guttering and smoking. Chemical dyes proved more satisfactory, but coloured candles are very much a twentieth-century phenomenon and the demand for more and varied colours gathered pace through the jazz age of the 1920s until today Price's of London, world famous candlemakers for 150 years, produce 24 different coloured candles. It is now possible to match or tone candles to almost any colour scheme including black, subtle greens or brilliant magenta. Decorative shapes, embossed and glittered, colour drip, spiralled, scented, tall and slim or short and fat candles are all available commercially. In recent years there has also been a revival of interest in handcrafted candles both dipped and moulded. It is possible to buy wax in bulk, wicks, dyes, moulds and scented crystals so that do-it-yourself enthusiasts can create candles with fantastic shapes, stripes, swirls and multi-colours.

They also provide a gently living flame which is all the more appealing in these days of central heating when we miss the flickering flames of open fires. From a design viewpoint they provide welcome vertical lines when almost everything else on a table is flat.

BUYING CANDLES

There is no one type of shop in which to look for candles. They turn up in unexpected places. I have even found unusual ones in a motorway service area shop. Stationers are the most likely source, as well as gift shops, craft shops,

departmental stores, even some bookshops and china shops. Specialist firms often have stalls or stands at large flower shows or exhibitions and at some county shows. Flower clubs may well have candles on their sales tables, especially near Christmas-time. Church furnishers are the people to go to for large, tall cream or white candles for special occasions.

Always check candles when you buy – for straightness (they may have been stored badly), colour fading or streaking, chipping and cracks. A faint horizontal hair-line crack may well be a complete break and a cracked candle is virtually impossible to repair satisfactorily.

If you are buying ordinary candles, rather than fancy, decorative ones, do not be mean about the length. Short dumpy ones will never have the elegance of longer ones and the difference in cost is little.

A covered base unites the two tall candles in candlesticks with the central arrangement. A soft coral colour in the flowers and the china is emphasized by candles and base of a slightly deeper coral

Long candles have an elegance which short ones lack. They make a small arrangement of late summer flowers look much more imposing than it would otherwise

Now that paper napkins are so attractive, practical and in general use for informal occasions, it is worth considering, when you buy candles, buying napkins of the same or toning colours. Even if not needed at once, they are an excellent standby in an emergency when unexpected guests catch you without fabric napkins to hand. With candles, toning napkins and a few flowers (real, or artificial ones kept for just such an occasion) an effective table can be quickly achieved.

FIXING CANDLES IN AN ARRANGEMENT

There are a number of satisfactory ways of securing candles:

1 Short or slim candles can simply be pushed into the *Oasis* until firmly held. Larger candles will sway and make a large hole so that they are never upright. It is better to use another method.

2 Use a small metal or plastic candle-holder (c or d) which can be bought from floral art suppliers or flower club sales tables. These are pushed down into the *Oasis* or onto the pinholder.

3 Use adhesive tape to fix four cocktail sticks or short lengths of stub wire (from a florist's) to the bottom of the candle (a). This is probably the most effective method if foam is being used as only the sticks or wires go into the block; the candle rests on the top. More room is left for the flowers and the foam is less likely to break up as a large hole is avoided. The tape and sticks are soon hidden by leaves and stems.

4 If a pinholder is being used, wrap the end of the candle in corrugated paper to give a better grip (b). Even if the paper is soaked with water it will hold well enough during a meal, though I would not trust this method for a show. In New Zealand I have seen hair-rollers used in a similar way.

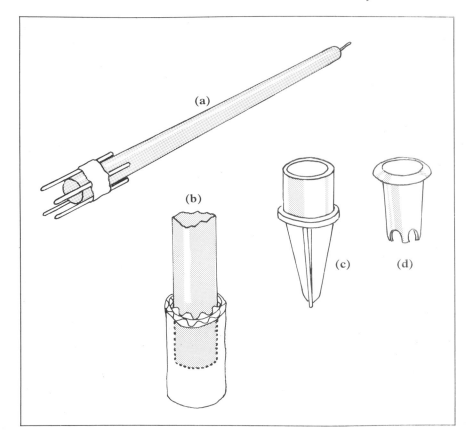

Ways of fixing candles: (a) Cocktail sticks taped to the end (b) Corrugated paper wound round the base (c) and (d) Two types of candle-holder which can be bought and used either with a pinholder or with floral foam

69

CANDLE-HOLDERS

Whether antique or modern, most candlesticks and candelabra have more or
less standard-sized holders and candles will fit quite well. If they do not:

a) Secure them with a blob or ring of putty-type adhesive.

b) Bind adhesive tape in a loose, crumpled bandage to the bottom inch of the
candle so that it fits more tightly into the socket.

c) Use the old-fashioned (but inclined to be messy) methods. Slightly melt the
bottom of a candle in a flame, push it into the holder and allow it to cool and
set, or, where a candlestick still holds the remains of a previous candle, light
the stub till the wax is molten, then press in the new candle to set in position.

Larger diameter candles are usually fixed onto a spike holder, but they can
equally well stand on a saucer, plate or other base secured with a generous knob
or ring of one of the putty-type adhesives. Empty wine or liqueur bottles make
attractive holders, too. Fill them first with water for stability before putting the
candle in the top.

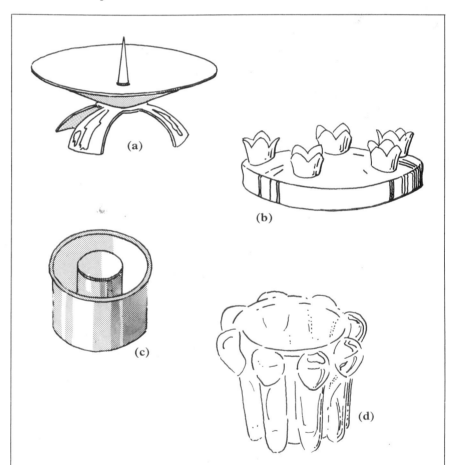

Different types of candle-
holders: (a) A spiked
holder, usually for a large
diameter candle (b) A base
to hold slim 'flowerlite'
candles (c) The tops of
some aerosol sprays with a
centre guard for the nozzle
make excellent emergency
holders (d) An inexpensive
glass holder widely
available

70

FIRE RISK

Be careful to see that plant material, especially any that is dried or artificial, does not come near a candle which is to be lit. Allow space for the candle to burn down during a meal and be sure that it is extinguished before everyone leaves the room. Lighted candles in an arrangement can be a fire risk unless care is taken.

If the candles are not to be lit, then lift the wicks upright and trim them if necessary.

Coffee by candlelight. The colours in the cups are repeated in the red-edged pelargoniums, antirrhinums and roses

For a teenage party wine bottles hold multi-coloured 'drip' candles with a very simple arrangement of yellow daisies

CHAPTER 6

On a Larger Scale

The best decorative effects are not necessarily, nor even probably, achieved by using rare or expensive flowers. . . . To some people it is still a matter for comment and surprise to find what really dramatic effects are to be achieved by the good use of the simplest flowers.
CONSTANCE SPRY, *Hostess*, 1961

ometimes flowers are needed for celebrations away from home. On these larger occasions everything is on a much bigger scale, if not in size, then in numbers. Flowers for such functions in hotels and banqueting rooms are usually arranged by professional florists, though in some hotels the task is carried out by their own staff. Learning to arrange the table flowers is part of a normal training in catering.

Economy Occasions

There are times when the amateur arranger is called on to undertake table decorations on a larger scale than usual; perhaps it is for the cricket (tennis, golf, sailing) club annual dinner, the old folks' Christmas luncheon, the Old Boys' (Girls') Reunion or a charity fund-raising function which can vary from a sit-down meal to a barbecue or a wine-and-cheese buffet. When these events are held in a hired, impersonal hall, they tend to be the Cinderellas of table decoration, devised at the last moment and carried out on a shoestring budget. Yet it need not be so, even in the difficult days of winter.

A certain amount of money must be allocated, of course. This can sometimes be wheedled out of the organizers or perhaps donated for a charity affair by an interested group such as the local flower club, horticultural society or Chamber of Commerce. It is not money wasted because the decorations can be sold or raffled at the end of the function and the cost recouped, or even a profit made to swell the funds.

PLANNING AN OVERALL SCHEME

It is important not to dot various little unrelated flower arrangements about the room on long or small individual tables. Plan an overall scheme, however simple, and stick to it. If its colours are to be red, white and blue, try to avoid

Restaurant flowers at Miss Cranston's Tearooms in Glasgow at the turn of the century. (*T. & R. Annan & Sons, Glasgow*)

unbalancing (even destroying) it by having to use yellow check tablecloths or orange-flowered china. The 'bitty' look destroys any feeling of harmony and as we have seen in the home it is repetition of a colour, a line, a style or a shape that gives unity to any design both in flower arrangement and the table setting. With an awkward colour scheme like red, white and blue it is better to let the red or the blue be the dominant colour and unifying factor. A patch of wrong colour, something in a different style, a conflicting line, destroys the rhythm which repetition always gives.

PREPARATION

Try to find out, before you even start planning the flowers, just what is available at the venue or being hired from elsewhere; how many people are expected; how many tables there will be and set out in what pattern; the type of meal; what lighting there is; whether flowers can be arranged at the venue or need to be brought already done.

CONTAINERS

If there are to be a large number of smallish arrangements down long dinner tables or on small individual ones, matching containers usually have to be provided and these can be from disposable or very inexpensive items, such as:

    margarine tubs (250g)

    yoghurt (150g) or cream (114ml) cartons

    polystyrene or hard plastic trays in which supermarket food is packed

    cooking foil trays and dishes

    plastic screw-tops from coffee jars

    ice-cream 'goblets'

    $7\frac{1}{2}$cm (3in.) plastic flower pots

    flower pot saucers

    scallop shells

    caps from aerosol spray cans

    small food tins, e.g. tuna, sardine, baked beans, ham, etc.

    plastic bottles which can easily be cut with scissors to make shallow watertight containers, e.g. from bleach, washing-up liquid, cooking oil, lemonade etc.

All these will hold water, though some will be very light and may need to have sand or gravel in the bottom to make them stable. Some can be used as they are; others, especially those with lettering, will need to be painted, either with emulsion or spray paints. Try to match your chosen colour scheme or choose a neutral earth-colour, grey or black, except perhaps for a wedding, when white or gold looks well. Metallic sprays are expensive but do save a lot of time and effort, whereas small tins of paint go a surprisingly long way.

MECHANICS

These can be one of the costliest items because plastic foam such as *Oasis* (either the green water-retaining type or brown for dried and artificial stems) is usually the quickest and most effective thing to use, but it is not cheap. Apart from saving time, it does eliminate spills.

FOLIAGE

Unless you have a great deal of time to spare for preparation go for long lasting evergreen foliages such as:

ivy	laurel (or bay)	cupressus
privet	mahonia	laurustinus
holly	skimmia	choisya

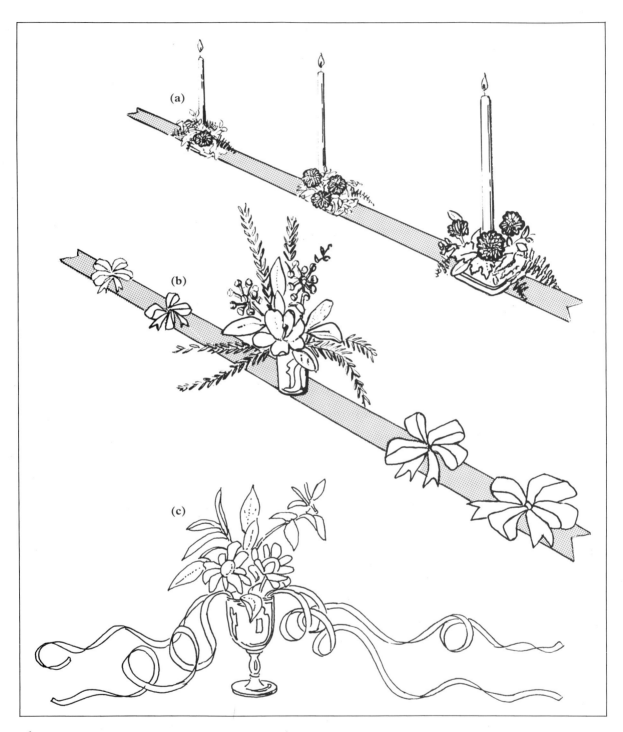

FLOWERS

These will depend on the time of year, but in spring, when inexpensive daffodils are plentiful, they make a good show; roses, at the right time, may be easy to get from gardens as may forsythia, blossom, Michaelmas daisies, bluebells, honesty and so on. Dahlias tend to be over-large for table-work, unless the smaller ones can be obtained. If one has to buy, then undoubtedly spray chrysanthemums and spray carnations give excellent value for money.

At Christmas and party-times artificial flowers made from paper or ribbon are acceptable substitutes. They should be well made and they have the advantage that any colour can be chosen to suit the occasion. Fruit seems an obvious choice to provide colour with reasonable economy, but from experience it disappears quite speedily from arrangements, leaving unsightly gaps!

RIBBONS

Florist's waterproof ribbon is inexpensive and available in a wide range of colours. It can be torn into narrow widths if needed. Loops, bows and streamers added to arrangements can replace or eke out a few flowers and make them look more lavish.

Ribbons can also be used as long runners down the centre of the table, secured at intervals to the cloth with small pieces of putty-type fixing material or double-sided adhesive tape. You can be quite inventive with variations on this theme, but it is essential, I think, to use a 'waterproof' material; crêpe-paper looks wretched with even one drop of liquid spilled on it and the dye can ruin a cloth underneath.

MOTIFS

If there is a motif associated with the club, organization, town or occasion this can well be incorporated into the decorative scheme. The drawings on page 78 give a few ideas. Very often the real thing (e.g. cricket stumps) is too large, but some can be 'translated' into plant material. White-painted dried stems of cow parsley or hogweed make excellent stumps and a red apple or red-painted gourd makes a good ball. Fixed in plasticine covered with moss and a little greenery added, they make an apt decoration for a cricket club dinner. Yacht sails are easily cut from thick paper or thin card, so are golf green pennants which can be wedged in a split garden cane. Footballs, tennis raquets, rugger balls can all be cut out of thick painted paper, wedged with plasticine or similar in a small plastic dish which will also hold a piece of *Oasis* for a little moss and

Left Use inexpensive waterproof ribbon from the florist to unify decoration on long tables: (a) A length of ribbon is fixed to the table with small arrangements in disposable polystyrene trays at intervals. Candles, even ordinary household ones, add to the festive look in the evening (b) If flowers are scarce and expensive decorate the ribbon runner with bows on either side of a central arrangement in a painted yoghurt pot (c) Curling ribbon streamers with their ends tucked into a wine-glass container make a few flowers look much more important

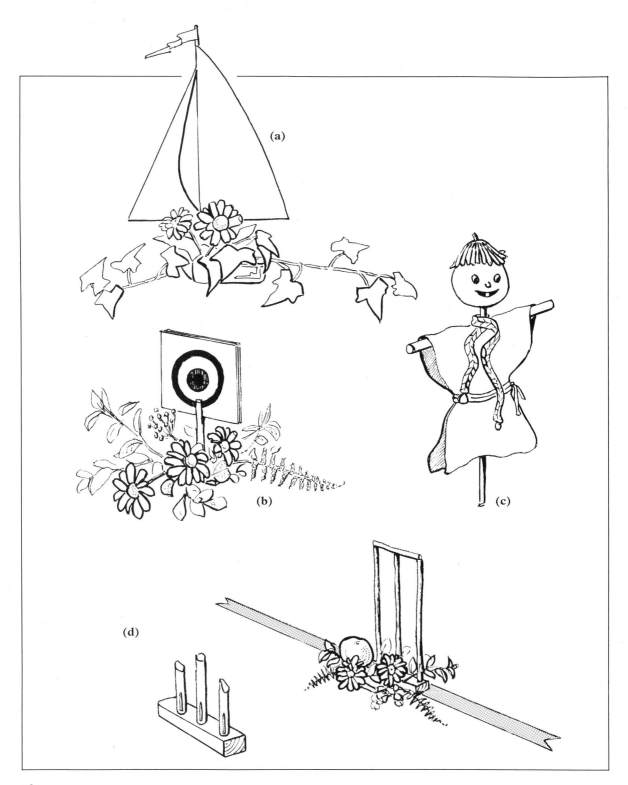

(a)

(b)

(c)

(d)

green leaves. Flowers are scarcely needed, though club colours can be picked up in them. Fish netting, shells and pebbles soon set a seaside theme and discarded cardboard rolls and tins build up easily into fantasy towers and buildings. Keep it simple; the secret is always to *repeat* the motif from the top table on the 'sprigs' or on the smaller tables about the room. This kind of table decoration makes the occasion special for those attending and is invariably appreciated. A little ingenuity and invention is worth far more than expensive flowers.

In Stately Homes

At the other extreme, as it were, from flowers in a bleak or utilitarian hall, amateur arrangers may find themselves taking part in a flower festival at a stately home where the dining-table is often featured as part of the tour of the house. Here there are priceless furnishings and *objets d'art* to set the scene and valuable carpets and polished surfaces to be protected.

ACQUIRING THE BACKGROUND INFORMATION

There are three ways of tackling the design for the table:

1 To try to do it entirely in period with the room. This may be difficult if the period is early (i.e. pre-Georgian) but even if not strictly followed the historical period can often suggest the manner of the decoration.

2 To link the table flowers to the colours and overall style of the room (e.g. severely classical, daintily rococo, fussily Victorian or exuberantly baroque), picking up either the principal colour of the room or emphasizing a smaller secondary hue to give contrast and impact.

3 To relate the flowers directly to the patterns and colours of the china, glass or table appointments. Although the table settings may be laid, almost in full (as it is one way to display the glass, porcelain and silver ware to visitors) the table cannot normally be treated as if it were really intended for seated guests. In a festival it has to be somewhat larger than life. The photograph of the tall cones at Lyme Park (page 81) is an excellent example.

Arrangers do not always plan their own decorations for an occasion like this and they may be given quite detailed designs by the festival designer. Or they may be given a general outline and asked to submit more detailed plans with sketches, listing the flowers and foliage they plan to use and their colours.

It is very important to look at the venue, and a viewing day is usually arranged by the organizers of the event. First impressions are important; let

Left Ideas for sports club functions and for Hallowe'en: (a) Cut-out paper sails and a pennant glued to a stick sail above ivy trails and flowers for a yacht club dinner (b) Rifle club targets held in a cleft stick can have the colours repeated in the flowers (c) For Hallowe'en a little apple-head guy made from crossed sticks and draped in a piece of sacking could be used instead (d) Stumps made from hollow dried stems impaled on nails in a wooden block make an effective wicket for a cricket club function. A shiny red apple or painted gourd can be included among the flowers (green and white, perhaps) to represent the ball

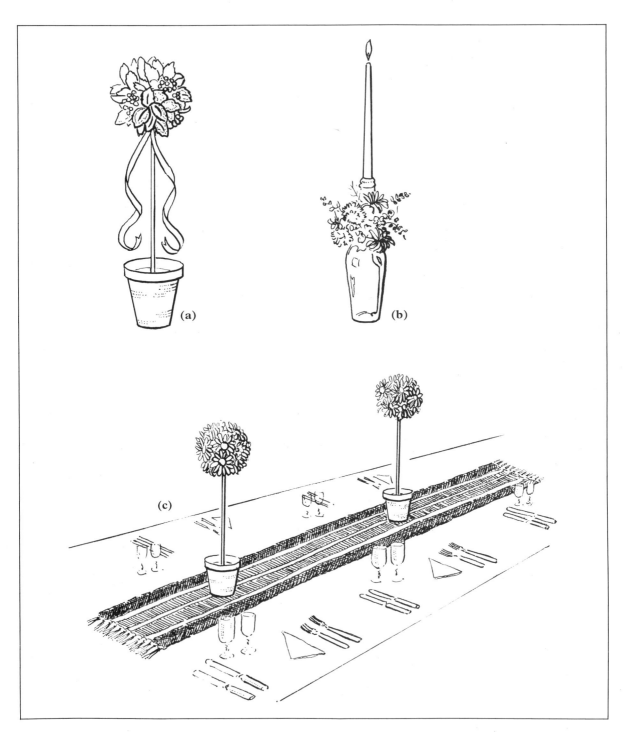

Left (a) A 'topiary' tree of evergreens and berries is made from a round of *Oasis* impaled on a cane set in plaster of Paris in a flower-pot. Curling ribbon streamers can be in a colour suitable for the event in question (b) Empty wine bottles in green or brown make good candle-holders. Slip half a round of *Oasis*, with a hole in the centre cut with an apple corer, over the bottle neck. Decorate this little collar with short sprigs of foliage and any flowers available. At Christmas time small baubles or ribbon bows are colourful (c) A school or college scarf makes a good table runner for a reunion dinner. Adhesive putty will keep it in place, stretched taut along the table. The topiary trees here can be in flowers to match one or more of the scarf colours

Below Towering cones of flowers, fruit and foliage at a flower festival at Lyme Park, Cheshire in 1975, designed by Bill Lomas. (*The Flower Arranger*)

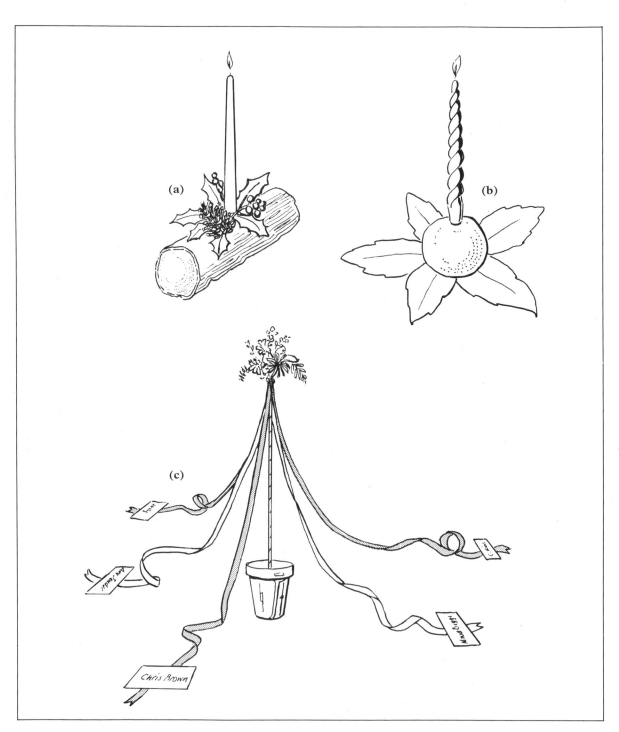

yourself absorb the atmosphere of the whole house first. Then concentrate on the dining-room or banqueting hall and let that sink in. Read the guidebook, research the history, then look again.

Now it is time to take copious notes and measurements; make sketches; take Polaroid photographs if allowed to; buy postcards if you can. Every detail is important and you will not remember the details next week unless you have an exceptional visual memory. Find out what may be used and what may not; what may be moved and what must remain exactly in its place; ask what else might be available for use. Take paint colour cards and mark the colours matching features in the room and on the table.

A painting by G. Clint, A.R.A., of the banquet given by the Corporation of London to the Prince Regent on 18 June 1814. (*Guildhall Art Gallery, City of London*)

Left (a) For Christmas a short log with a hole drilled to take a candle can be simply decorated with holly and cones pressed into a knob of plasticine. Artificial snow or white shoe-cleaner will give more atmosphere (b) A cored apple makes a good candle-holder. Stand it on a star made from five laurel or aucuba leaves (c) Make a flower top-knot for a maypole with ribbon streamers to placecards

THE DETAILED DESIGN

Then, and only then, are you ready to design and plan. Recall your first impressions and thoughts; they may still be the best ideas, but they must be considered objectively and with a mind open to other ideas and suggestions from those working with you as a team. Economy will probably not be your first consideration, but your budget must be kept fully in mind.

Many such festivals are planned a year ahead of the event and if viewing can be at the same time of the year as the festival it is a great help because you will see the sort of light and atmosphere you can expect (though this is far from certain in Britain!) and can check positively on the plant material likely to be available. Some can even be grown specially in the year ahead.

Because in stately homes there is likely to be a great deal of other beauty around in pictures, fabrics, carvings, tapestries, porcelain, glass and so on, a table decoration needs to have a kind of simply stated grandeur. Even if it is to be cluttered and trailing and posied in Victorian glory, it will need to be a refinement of the style, a kind of mild caricature to give it impact on a grander scale.

Assess what flowers and foliage are needed and the colours and numbers of each, remembering that because a table is bigger it doesn't necessarily need *more* flowers and leaves, but it will need *larger* ones than you normally use on your dining-table at home. Bold fruits such as pineapples and large leaves like artichokes can be used in a way they never could in smaller rooms.

It is a wonderful opportunity to work amongst beautiful things, whether on a truly baroque scale or in more simple medieval style. Even if you doubt your own ability to do justice to such settings, never turn down the opportunity to help a more experienced arranger or to be one of a team. There will be willing hands to help you and it will be an experience to treasure.

Flowers arranged on a *surtout* in the Canaletto Room for the NAFAS Festival of Flowers in Woburn Abbey in 1968. Arrangers: Mrs Mary Barnard and Mrs Dora Buckingham (*NAFAS*)

The table in the State Dining Room at Woburn Abbey decorated by arrangers from flower clubs in the North Midlands for a festival. (*NAFAS*)

Below 'The Mayor's Banquet' at the NAFAS Festival 1979. Arranger: Susan Phillips (*NAFAS*)

A table arrangement that is typical of the period at the Royal Horticultural
Society's Show in 1906. Arranged by Frances Jeanette Roelink. (Photograph lent
by the arranger's grand-daughter, Pamela Hannon)

CHAPTER 7

Table Classes in Shows

Take the class for Table Decoration (and no show can keep the public interest alive without these Decorative Sections), and you will find that most societies have various restrictions which cramp competitors' work and should be done away with.
R.F. FELTON, *British Floral Decoration*, 1910

History of Table Classes in Shows

nterest in table decoration classes at the Royal Horticultural Society Shows and at horticultural and county shows in Britain began in the last quarter of the nineteenth century. At first it was the gardener who competed since it was his task to provide and arrange the floral decorations indoors. The lady of the house might 'direct' the staging of the competitive entry. Later on others took part, professionals and non-professionals who enjoyed working with flowers.

One of these was Miss Annie Hassard of Norwood, who in 1870 wrote one of the earliest Victorian flower arrangement books, *Floral Decoration in Dwelling Houses*. Her work was described by the press as 'exquisitely airy and refined'. The work of Mr Cyphers of Cheltenham who was exhibiting in the same period, was said to be 'dashing, precise and hard, as befits a man'. His prize-winning table at a Birmingham Royal Horticultural Society Show in 1873 used 'three brilliantly shining glass epergnes' with multi-coloured flowers, pink heaths, pink and white roses, grasses and ferns. With these he staged a set of small matching vases of scarlet geraniums, white eucharist lilies and red roses.

Interest in show tables continued unabated during the Edwardian period. Between 1903 and 1914, Mrs Frances Roelink was an exhibitor who achieved success with table arrangements at the Crystal Palace and Royal Horticultural Society Shows. The picture shows a 1906 summer arrangement of roses in an epergne with two smaller vases on a tablecloth decorated with crochet lace edging and corners, but no table appointments are included.

At that time it was customary to treat a small show table (often only a cloth-covered card table) as if it were the centre area of a large dining table. The centre-piece and corners were usually linked with trailing fern, smilax, selaginella, clematis or rose foliage, and quite often there would be another

A table class at Taunton
Flower Show, 1981

little vase halfway along. White cloths were obligatory and no china, glass or cutlery permitted.

Miss Violet Stevenson's winning table decoration at a National Carnation Show just before World War II was a low central arrangement of carnations and their own foliage, with two smaller bowls in a diagonal line. At that time this 'homely' approach was most unusual.

In the 1950s when flower clubs were just starting to be formed, coloured cloths gradually came to be used but settings with china and glass were still fairly rare and at the first Flower Arrangement Academy in London in 1952 this was still so. By the time the National Association of Flower Arrangement Societies was formed in 1959, tables at shows were beginning to look more like real dinner or luncheon tables with laid place settings and sometimes even cutlery. They were often trestles, usually 2 metres (6 feet) long by about 1 metre (3 feet) wide. For example, the schedule for the table class at the NAFAS 1961 competition, reads:

Class 7 'Dinner Party' – A table decorated with fresh plant material for a summer dinner party using a cloth or other covering and showing place settings. Any accessories may be used but no cutlery. The size of the table will be approximately 6ft × 3ft.

Since then table classes have appeared in many NAFAS national competitions, roughly in alternate years. County and horticultural shows have also included table decorations for a long, long time. Taunton Flower Show, for example, still has three large table classes which are a pleasure to judge. Shrewsbury is another show which preserves the table tradition and the City of Leicester Show still includes two classes with a note in the schedule that they are 'judged by points for lightness, harmony of colour and originality of arrangement'.

One of the tables at
Taunton Flower Show,
1981

Table Classes in Flower Shows Today

Today standards of presentation in table classes are very high, and showing can
be quite expensive as the exhibitor has to provide not only the flowers, but also
the table coverings. It has become almost *de rigueur* to have the table covering
tailored perfectly, often gathered or mitred to fit, finished with cording, swags,
tassels or overlays as appropriate to the theme. The result is often superb, but
the coverings may possibly never be used again since table sizes vary from show
to show and with this kind of finish one inch of difference can be enough to
make a previously used cloth quite useless.

There is also the matter of interpretation. Now that it is usual to have a class
title for the table decorations there is a tendency for these to be of the grander
occasion sort: 'Jubilee Celebrations', 'Stately Home', 'Glittering Occasion' or
'Civic Reception'. All of them call for fine table appointments that few
competitors may have or be able to borrow. Even if they are available, now that
even minor antiques are valuable there may be fear of theft if the class is not
closely stewarded. A more realistic approach was 'Pot Luck – an informal
buffet table exhibit' at the NAFAS Festival 1980.

Table decorations are as much enjoyed by visitors and viewers today as they
have ever been.

89

The Kent Area Show,
1981, at Tonbridge
School. Exhibits in the
buffet table class
'Glittering Occasion':
a) First prize and Best in
Show award: Mrs Pat
Williams
b) Second prize: Mrs
Barbara Mallard
c) Mrs Joan Dugay's
exhibit

(a)

(b)

(c)

Guidelines for Competitors

THE SCHEDULE

In any competitive work the schedule is of the first importance. It will contain all the exhibitor needs to know about the title or theme, the size of the table, whether it is to be viewed from all round and if coverings are provided, what plant materials may be used and whether accessories and cutlery are permitted. But there may also be some 'unseen' rules in the form of a reference to judging in accordance with such and such a handbook or manual. This will be just as important as the show schedule itself, and it is essential to obtain a copy if such a book is mentioned. In the United Kingdom most (though not all) flower arrangement shows today are judged in accordance with the *NAFAS Handbook of Schedule Definitions*, Seventh edition, 1982.★

The *NAFAS Handbook of Schedule Definitions* clearly states that:

> Table exhibits are presented for decoration and not necessarily for functional use. Accessories may always be used unless specifically prohibited . . . but plant material must predominate over all other components used. . . . All tables, with the exception of the buffet style, must be judged from a seated as well as a standing position.

This is much more generous advice than earlier versions of the booklet have given, and it is now clear that the exhibitor has a great deal of freedom in laying out a table. China, cutlery, napkins and accessories can be used to make a decorative pattern as a setting for the flower arrangement; overcrowding can be avoided and the best possible use made of colour which can be better balanced if it does not have to be dotted about the table.

Under the heading 'Tables', the *NAFAS Judges' Manual* gives further excellent advice for judge and competitor:

> Plant material should be in perfect condition, with no offensive smelling flowers or foliage. Cloth and accessories should be appropriate for the type of meal, immaculately pressed and clean. Care must be taken that the plant material is not dominated by accessories. . . .
>
> *Luncheon* tables should normally be a little informal regarding design, cloth and setting.
>
> *Dinner* tables are usually more formal . . . and the plant material more elegant than for a luncheon party. The height of the decoration should be such that from a seated position it is possible to hold conversation across the table, either over, through, below or to the side of the placements of plant material.
>
> *Buffet* tables require placements of plant material which are bold and eye-catching, and which are stable to withstand jostling. . . . Originality for a

---

★ A copy of this small booklet is obtainable from NAFAS Publications, 21a Denbigh Street, London SW1V 2HF, price (in 1982) 25 pence, plus postage.

party is very suitable and may be achieved with ingenious accessories. . . .
Buffet table arrangements need not necessarily be required to be seen all
round, and may be allocated niched positions.

With so much good advice the competitor should not go far wrong, but there
are one or two tips still worth adding.

CANDLES

Candles are accessories even if they are actually placed *in* the arrangement
among the flowers and leaves. Before planning to use them make certain that
accessories are permitted by the actual schedule. Fix them as securely as
possible and make sure they are vertical. Drunken-looking candles can ruin a
lovely table. Unfortunately they are easily set askew by a knock to the table
during staging or judging, though an open table class area is usually cordoned
off before the public comes in.

It is customary in the United Kingdom for candles to be unlit and for the
wicks to be unburned. Sometimes they are glittered for party tables and
occasionally a false 'flame' is added of paper, foil or card. If wicks are left in
their natural state, they should be tweaked upright and trimmed with a sharp
pair of scissors. Don't leave the wick drooping sadly over the candle.

DOMINANCE OF PLANT MATERIAL

This is not normally a problem when a small table is provided, but when it is a 2
metre × 1 metre (6 feet × 3 feet) trestle the actual arrangement(s) have a lot of
flat table surface to compete with. The present day preference for low
arrangements accentuates the difficulty and using many accessories to break up
the surface area merely aggravates the problem. So when planning a large show
table remember that:

1 Very light-coloured cloths will be more dominant than darker ones. White
cloths are the most difficult of all to use, but strong bright colours can be
equally eye-catching. Muted or greyed tones may be safer.
2 Slightly shiny textures will be more dominant than matt surfaces; so will
patterns, even quite small all-over designs.
3 It will help if there is more than one arrangement, but be sure they have a
common feature with some plant materials, colours or shapes repeated in all of
them.
4 If the arrangements are low, try to include some vertical features such as
candles, bottles, decanters, figurines or tall glasses to break up the horizontal
expanse of cloth. Don't overdo it or the accessories will become dominant
themselves.

TABLE LINEN

If a table has a full length skirt, the fabric should be about 2.5cm (1in.) from the
floor, not touching, to allow it to hang well. When a throwover cloth is used the
overhang should, ideally, be level all round. All possible creases should be
eliminated, but a centre fold lengthways is acceptable on a long table. For really

Best in Show winner at the Harrogate Spring Show 1975: 'Galloping Gourmet' by Mrs Beryl Gray. (*The Flower Arranger*)

formal tables napkins should be of fabric, folded and displayed in a way that suits the style of the table. In Britain paper napkins are accepted for informal occasions. Place mats should be in proportion to the size of the table and should not overlap each other. Ideally places should be laid with the centre of one about 50–60cm (20–24in.) from the centre of the next, but space does not always allow this.

PLACE SETTINGS

All plates, cutlery and mats should be lined up equidistant from the edge of the table – about 2·5cm (1in.) in is usually right if the table is laid in a functional manner. Avoid too much clutter and take away some items that might normally be used if it begins to look overcrowded.

FOOD

Apart from whole vegetables and fruits used decoratively food is best avoided on show tables. Occasionally one sees bread rolls, crispbread, coffee mints, petit fours and sugar, but since nothing looks worse than dry or moisture sweating foods, it is better to leave them out.

OVERALL STYLE

The judge will be looking for an overall style, character or quality in the table so that linen, china and flowers are suited to each other, to the class title and to the occasion or the meal in question. The Victorians might have said 'so that it is all in good taste'. Today we are less inclined to bandy about the phrase 'good taste' because it means so many different things to people of differing race, religion, culture, age or social standing. Nevertheless, we can recognize the unifying qualities of line, colour, texture and character, and the really good table decoration with distinction will have them. Generally speaking, the more formal the occasion, the finer and smoother will be the textures of all the items used, including the flowers, fruit or foliage. Informality is likely to be suggested by the rougher textures of hand-thrown pottery, basketware, natural wood, coarse-woven fabrics and bolder plant material.

International Competitions

In recent years, international judging and competing have increased enormously. With the foundation in 1981 of a World Association of Flower Arrangers (WAFA) international competition is bound to increase still further. The World Association will have its own rules for the shows it organizes, in whatever country they are held, and because of the difficulties of accurate translation, these rules will be simple and brief. Individual countries, however, are likely to continue to have their own rules for their own shows.

The globe-trotting competitor, or judge, will find many variations in local rules for table classes and it will be wise to take local advice and remember too, that traditions, attitudes and conventions will certainly vary from those at home. Judging concepts and ethics may also be quite different. What is accepted in one country may be seen quite differently in another. Australia, Belgium, Bermuda, France, Italy, Monaco, Natal, New Zealand, Zimbabwe and many other countries have their own rules and advice to offer about competition tables.

The American System

In the USA the National Council of State Garden Clubs recognizes three different types of table classes at shows:

1 **A functional table** which is logically set for the service of food and is fully set with the exception of cutlery/silverware. Such tables may be formal (in which case symmetry of design is essential), semi-formal, or informal, as the schedule requires;

2 **An exhibition table** is a display for decorative effect and not arranged for logical use. Plates, for example, may be displayed vertically and napkins grouped as a colour unit;

3 **A segment table** is a capsulized version of a full table and may be either functional or exhibition as the schedule states.

A *functional segment* usually displays one place setting in a logical manner, with a cloth or mat and a decoration of plant material and accessories as needed.

An *exhibition segment* is a purely decorative arrangment of table items where the cloth perhaps is used as a background or drape, the flower arrangement(s) raised at different levels, a glass lying on its side and so on. Such displays are popular with viewers as they give ideas of colour combinations and accessories which can be used for a full table at home.

It is this third 'segment' class which could be far more widely used in Britain. For show organizers it has the advantage of taking up less space and for the competitors it is much less demanding on the pocket and other resources.

Esther Veramae Hame'l, in her book *The Encyclopaedia of Judging and Exhibiting* gives much detailed, specific and valuable advice to competitors and judges in the United States Garden Club shows. She stresses particularly that exhibition segments should not be so impractical that all impression of dining is lost, and emphasizes throughout that the textural character and colour relationships of any table must produce overall harmony, however informal the table may be. Mrs Hame'l gives some keywords to help both judge and exhibitor to gauge the success of a table decoration. Formal tables, she says, should be symmetrical, dignified, elegant and impeccable; semi-formal tables are only slightly less elegant and may involve some asymmetry, but informal tables should be creative, stimulating, stylish, striking, relaxed and friendly.

Looking to the Future

With such a distinguished history and world-wide interest, it would indeed be sad if table classes at shows died out in Britain. If the USA 'segment table' were adopted there could well be a revival of interest from show organizers and competitors. Niches, common at most flower arrangement shows in Britain, could be used for both buffet-style and for exhibition segments, but they are usually much too high for a functional segment as such settings are mostly flat and the upper area of the niche would not be used. For these, table top spaces, with fairly low divisions between competitors, would look best.

Titles for table classes could be more carefully chosen to give scope for table appointments that are more easily obtainable than precious silver, cut glass and antique candelabra. It is not often that one comes across a really up-to-date decoration designed for a modern table with chunky oven-to-table ware and stainless steel or wooden-handled cutlery. Our eating habits are far less formal than they were even ten years ago, and this should be reflected in show class titles. Here are a few suggestions, taken from schedules the world over:

Pot Luck	Informal supper table decoration
Patio Party	
Alfresco	Garden table for supper outdoors
Meal on the Moon	
Supper in Space	Imaginative table setting for the Space Age
Colour it Red/Blue/Green	Table decoration with one dominant colour
Romance and Roses	Tête-à-tête supper table
Seafood Supper	Decoration for a fish meal
Kiddies' Corner	Sit-down table for a five-year-old's birthday
House-warming	Newly-weds' informal party table
Bistro	Decoration for a meal with a French flavour
Flamenco	Decoration for a meal with a Spanish flavour
Bouzouki	Decoration for a meal with a Greek flavour
Après ski	For a meal at the end of an active day
Carol Singers' Cheer	Buffet table to warm and welcome
Ploughman's Lunch	Wine and cheese luncheon table
Just the Family	Very informal sit-down evening meal
Thé Dansant	1930s tea table decoration
Come and Get It	Decoration for a serving table in the kitchen
Video Victuals	
Commercial Break	Informal buffet for the long TV session

CHAPTER 8

Hostess in a Hurry

. . . if restraint is called for anywhere in flower treatment, it is surely here;
and nowhere is simplicity of arrangement so desirable, or so truly welcome, as
in the decoration of a dinner-table.
R.P. BROTHERSTON, *The Book of Cut Flowers*, 1906

he traditional family dining-room where everyone assembled for meals has all but disappeared in this country since World War II. Where it exists as a separate room (in less than a quarter of homes in Britain) it is likely to be quite small. More often today the dining area is either part of the single living-room or the kitchen. The dining-table itself will not be large and will do double duty throughout the day as a surface for brick-building, model-making, homework, dress-making or typing.

Many families today hardly ever sit down for a meal together. They arrive in relays according to their various activities and timetables, grabbing a snack or a sandwich almost on the run. Television has wooed us away from the dining-table to meals on card tables and trays. It is probable, then, that most of us arrange flowers for the meal table only for special occasions or when we have friends or guests for a meal. But what of ourselves and our families? May we not have the pleasure of a flower decoration on the table every day, or at least every weekend? Too much of a chore? Too expensive? Too little time? None of these is really true.

The cost can be small, even today, for those with just the tiniest garden. Thought and ingenuity count far more than expensive flowers. If you consider the additional possibilities of foliage, seedheads, berries, fruit and wood together with accessories such as candles, shells, figurines and other ornaments the variations are many. Don't try to be too elaborate; since the area on the table available for flowers is likely to be small, surprisingly few flowers and leaves will be needed.

In giving on the following pages an idea for every week of the year I have tried to suggest only the simplest of containers which anyone may have, or could buy inexpensively, and easily available plant materials. If you do not have the exact ones, think of similar shapes and colours. Obviously seasons vary from year to year and what may be available in mid-March this year, may

Mauve honesty flowers and Queen Anne's lace in a pewter mug to greet a guest for tea

not be out until April of next. The list is intended to spark off ideas to develop your own seeing eye and mind, so that your table need never be without a 'flower arrangment' of some kind, even if there is no flower in it! To quote from the NAFAS booklet on table decoration, an arrangement will

welcome a guest;
brighten a dull day;
add importance to a simple meal;
highlight a special occasion;
make a talking point at meal times.

Flowers are 'the smile on your table' – keep that smile welcoming.

Candles, real or artificial fruit and a leaf or two on a woven rush mat

A Year's Supply of Ideas – one for each week

Month and week	Container/base	Arrangement
1 January 1st week	(See 4th week in December) Small round ceramic dish to hold a round of *Oasis*. Stand it on round base made by covering a cake-board with gold/yellow fabric.	Re-use the holly, ivy and artificial Christmas roses, but remove all the red items. Instead add two or three small lemons or tangerines mounted on cocktail sticks.

A few anemones and freesias with ivy sprays (*The Bulb Information Desk*)

Month and week	Container/base	Arrangement
2 January 2nd week	Low woven basket, old meat dish or deep soup plate.	A deep fruit bowl hides most of the colourful fruit. Try using a flattish container. Add one or two evergreen leaves such as laurel or aucuba. If fruit is very expensive, crumple paper to take up some of the depth.
3 January 3rd week	Large sugar basin, vegetable or soup tureen, fruit bowl or casserole dish.	Dig up a small clump of snowdrops and plant them in a bowl. Moss looks well covering the soil and conserves moisture.
4 January 4th week	A blue bowl, red glass dish or tin painted or covered with fabric to match one of the flower colours.	Anemones are usually sold in mixed-colour bunches – use them this way but 'play up' one of the colours with the container.
5 January 5th week	Low pottery dish with *Oasis* block.	Just two (even one if it is generous) sprays of chrysanthemums from the florist can be cut carefully to make a low arrangement with evergreen leaves – holly, cypressus, choisya, skimmia, ivy, laurustinus.
6 February 1st week	Candlestick fitted with a matching (or painted to match) candlecup.	The green-to-black berries of tree ivy are most decorative. Arrange them with trails of ivy leaves including some variegated ones if possible.

Different ivies arranged in a red and green bowl from the tea service

Month and week	Container/base	Arrangement
7 February 2nd week	A shallow bowl or earthenware dish with a pinholder.	Forsythia cut now and brought indoors will open within a week. Cut four or five sprays and add a bunch of daffodils from the florist or enjoy the forsythia alone.
8 February 3rd week	As last week, or a tall jug.	Branches of pear or flowering currant cut now will open indoors. Add tulips or freesias if you wish.
9 February 4th week	An earthenware or plain coloured jug or tall vase.	Pussy willow is gleaming silver in the hedgerows. Cut some now to enjoy its opening indoors.
10 March 1st week	Dish, soup plate or tin tray.	Try a plate garden; children can do this. Fill a dish with moss and hide a small pinholder to hold a twig for a tree. Add stones. Tuck in small spring flowers to look as if they are growing in clumps.
11 March 2nd week	A shallow bowl with a pinholder.	Mimosa is in the shops now and likes a moist atmosphere so arrange it with an expanse of water. Cover the pinholder with attractive pebbles.
12 March 3rd week	A small bulb bowl, sugar or gravy tureen, casserole or plastic lined basket – if the latter, leave the handle free.	Arrange a multi-coloured mixture of any spring flowers available – even one of a kind will add to the tapestry effect.
13 March 4th week	Small deep bowl.	A growing clump of primroses, polyanthus or crocus will transplant from the garden. If you can, match colours with the bowl.
14 March 5th week	Vase or jug.	Daffodils never look as well as when bunched in a vase or jug with their own leaves. Mix all kinds. Cut stem lengths so that heads are on different levels.

Right Daffodils and pussy willow look well in a shallow container with an expanse of water showing

Month and week		Container/base	Arrangement
15	April 1st week	Shallow bowl with pinholder – or an old-fashioned glass 'rose'.	Tulips as they open bend and twist in attractive curves. Loop some of the leaves into 'bows' to cover the pinholder.
16	April 2nd week	Shallow bowl and pinholder.	If you, or a friend, can spare a spray or two from a magnolia tree, enjoy watching the waxen petals opening indoors.
17	April 3rd week	Low bowl – black is ideal – with pinholder.	The flowers of the large trees are often forgotten. Black ash buds break into purplish-black flower clusters at this time. Arrange with a few bright flowers.
18	April 4th week	Three to five egg-cups, small coffee cups or small pots, preferably matching, grouped on a circular base.	Group one type of small flower in each pot – primroses, violets, primulas, heather, grape hyacinths – as a cluster of colours and textures.
19	May 1st week	Bowl or jug.	Spires of honesty (lunaria) in purple, mauve and white make good cut flowers. Leave some for 'silver penny' seed-heads later on.
20	May 2nd week	Bowl, jug or basket.	Wallflowers are rich and velvety and smell sweetly. They are best 'unarranged'. If cut with some woody stem they last longer.
21	May 3rd week	Low bowl with pinholder.	Late double tulips have quite a different character from the singles. They combine well with blossom or with rough textured wood.
22	May 4th week	Low bowl or dish with pinholder.	Apple blossom – three or four short branches in bud fixed oriental-fashion on a pinholder to make a low, open arrangement. Add leaves, pinks, tulips or other available flowers if desired.

Month and week	Container/base	Arrangement
23 June 1st week	Tall narrow-necked vase – ceramic, glass, metal or wood – or use a liqueur bottle.	Collect flowering grasses – any grasses. Bunch them in the hand with heads at different levels, tie them with wool or use a rubber band, then slip them into a narrow-necked vase.
24 June 2nd week	Silver or glass container.	The old-fashioned pinks like 'Mrs Sinkins' are mostly enjoyed for their scent, but also provide an attractive bowl of rough-textured petals.
25 June 3rd week	Shallow bowl, preferably black – or paint an old soup plate.	Float three or four rose heads of the same or similar colour, with one or two leaves in 1930s fashion.
26 June 4th week	Small woven basket – tin or plastic lining. Wire mesh to fix flowers.	Three, five or more roses and buds arranged casually with wire mesh as support. Use a larger basket if you have plenty of roses.
27 July 1st week	Any container.	Alchemilla is a true flower arranger's flower. Lime-green frothy heads are dainty alone, combine with anything, dry well and will take up glycerine solution.
28 July 2nd week	Glass or silver container.	Sweet peas arrange themselves. Bunch them in single or mixed colours and simply drop them into a bowl or vase. Lift a few stems to avoid a too-flat look.
29 July 3rd week	A tall cherub container or candlestick with cup.	Modern pinks, such as 'Doris' which can be bought from the florist, combine well with roses and are long lasting as buds will open to replace faded flowers.
30 July 4th week	A figurine, small container and a base to stand both on.	If you have a china figurine look out for small flowers and leaves in the same colours. Arrange these to complement the figure.

Blue love-in-a-mist in a green dumpy wine bottle would suit a picnic in the garden

Month and week	Container/base	Arrangement
31 August 1st week	Black bowl with a pinholder and/or crumpled wire mesh.	White daisies (marguerites) are distinctive arranged in a black container. Cut the stems different lengths and turn the heads in every direction.
32 August 2nd week	Plate, cakestand or plastic urn.	While white daisies are plentiful cover a cone-shaped block of soaked *Oasis* with short-stemmed (about 2cm – 1in.) flower heads.
33 August 3rd week	Low bowl or dish.	Gladioli as spikes are too large for most tables, but separate florets look well floating in a shallow dish.
34 August 4th week	Large sea-shell.	Wedge a piece of water-soaked foam into the shell and prop it up at a pleasing angle. Arrange a few petunias, nasturtiums, antirrhinums or roses to spill casually out of the shell.

Month and week	Container/base	Arrangement
35 August 5th week	Low black bowl or pewter plate.	Two or three vivid geranium flower heads floating with a leaf or two.
36 September 1st week	Hessian-covered base with small painted tin for a pinholder.	A twist of stripped ivy or dried wood of interesting texture with just two brightly-coloured dahlias, roses or geraniums at the base.
37 September 2nd week	As last week.	Fix the stripped ivy or wood horizontally this time and use two other flowers of different colour.
38 September 3rd week	Any type of container, high or low.	My own favourite table-piece: a collection of bits and pieces – leaves, berries, seedheads – whatever is about. Try to find a linking colour which will unify them.
39 September 4th week	Figurine container or candlestick with candlecup.	Variegated honeysuckle or ivy leaves with just a few berries from garden or hedgerow.

Petunias, ivy, love-in-a-mist and blue-green leaves of rue pick up the mother-of-pearl colouring of the shell container

Month and week	Container/base	Arrangement
40 October 1st week	Low bowl or basket.	Rosy apples with a late rose or two in a cigar tube of water tucked between them.
41 October 2nd week	Raised container or small dish on a hessian-covered base.	Glycerined beech leaves with a few orange or yellow dahlias.
42 October 3rd week	Green or metal container.	An arrangement of leaves only. Look for varying shapes – strap-shaped, ferns, cupressus, laurel, ivy, lonicera, box. Have at least three or four different shapes and different greens.
43 October 4th week	Shallow basket or tray.	It is often possible to buy gourds – yellow, warty, green and white, striped, mottled. Cluster them in a shallow container with an evergreen leaf or two.
44 November 1st week	Small wooden box, jewel casket or lidded basket with plastic container inside fitted with *Oasis*.	Unless there have been early frosts there will still be odd sprays, berries and small flowers left in the garden. Prop the box or basket lid half-open with a short stick. In this way very few flowers are needed to make an attractive arrangement.
45 November 2nd week	Place mat or fabric-covered base.	Now is the time to resort to bunches of plastic grapes (very realistic). Fix two candles at slightly unequal heights in low holders. Group, say, four bunches of grapes round them. Add leaves – or ribbon bows for a party meal.
46 November 3rd week	Polished wood slice.	Into a knob of plasticine push a few dried or glycerine-preserved leaves and a cluster of fir cones or seed heads such as teasels.

Right Artificial flowers of blue and beige in an unusual container add colour to the children's high-tea table

Month and week	Container/base	Arrangement
47 November 4th week	Round dish with round of *Oasis*.	By now berried holly is usually at its best. Pick some ready for Christmas and lay it on the ground in the garden. Use a few sprays of berries stripped of all leaves to brighten an arrangement of leaves.
48 December 1st week	White painted circular or oval base – plasticine to fix flowers.	Find time to paint with white matt paint some cheap plastic flowers and leaves and a circular oval wood base. Arrange these in a low arrangement, then spray the whole thing with gloss paint to look like white china.
49 December 2nd week	As last week.	Add two candles in white candleholders, perhaps combined with the white arrangement on an oval base covered to suit the room decor.
50 December 3rd week	White urn/vase with pinholder and wire mesh.	If you have snowberries nearby, a tallish white urn arranged with stems of them, stripped of leaves and arching over like a fountain, needs nothing added.
51 December 4th week	Small bowl on a covered base.	No doubt you plan something special for Christmas but meanwhile use holly and cupressus with real or artificial berries and artificial Christmas roses for an arrangement to last up to Christmas Eve.
52 December 5th week	As last week.	Be ready to greet the New Year. Whilst out over the holiday look for budding hazel or alder catkins and pussy willow. They can all be forced indoors.

Left Brown and black baskets from New Zealand arranged with brown artificial roses, rhododendron leaves with suede-like texture and black painted hollow stems which suit a modern setting

Appendix

GUIDELINES FOR THE NEWCOMER TO FLOWER ARRANGING

The newcomer should not be put off by the mystique that has grown up around flower arranging in the past few years. Basically the craft is a simple one, but as with all hobbies and occupations, the right equipment and a little knowhow make the whole thing easier and much, much more interesting. There are many books which the beginner can consult, but for those new to table decoration, the following hints will be useful.

Containers

Virtually anything can be used nowadays as a receptacle for flowers. If it does not naturally hold water (e.g. a basket, box or hollowed-out piece of driftwood) then a small bowl, tin or plastic carton can be placed inside to form the actual container for water and the plant material.

Candlecups in metal or plastic can be bought inexpensively from a florist or garden centre to convert a candlestick, candelabra, bottle or tall narrow-necked vase into a useful flower container. To secure the candlecup into the neck or socket use a putty-type adhesive such as *Oasisfix*, *Plasticine* or strip *Bostik*.

Most beginners choose a container which is too large and too deep. This often overwhelms the plant material they have available and makes the arranging much more difficult. With modern 'mechanics' (see following section) quite shallow bowl-shaped containers can be used. For the long, low type of table arrangement which is going to be about 60cm (24in.) long and 25cm (10in.) wide when finished, a 15cm (6in.) long container is quite large enough unless it is very decorative and will play an important part in the design. For a small round arrangement about 30cm (12in.) in diameter, a dish 10cm (4in.) in diameter is about the right size.

Supports for Stems – 'Mechanics'

For good designing and arranging, stems need to be supported exactly where you want them, and not move. Nowadays arrangers use three different forms of support:

1 A pinholder (also called a needlepoint holder or kenzan).
2 Crumpled wire netting of about 5cm (2in.) mesh.
3 Floral foam such as *Oasis*, *Aquarius*, *Bloomfix* or *Florafoam*. The green foam

blocks, when soaked, hold a large quantity of water for fresh plant material; the fawn and brown foams do *not* hold water and are for use with dried, preserved or artificial stems.

The diagrams show how each of these mechanics should be used.

For low arrangements:

1 A pinholder should be secured to the bottom of a *dry* container with three 'pills' or a ring of putty-type adhesive. Make sure it is quite secure by giving the pinholder a twist as though tightening a screw-top jar. Pinholders support branches and thick stems quite securely on the pins, but are less effective for very thin stems which slip between the pins.

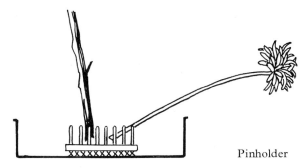

Pinholder

2 Crumpled wire netting must be domed up above the top of the container to be really effective. There should be three or more layers of holes to support stems. Secure the netting with crossed rubber bands, or tie it with string like a parcel, or use crossed adhesive tape in the same way. Floral tape can be

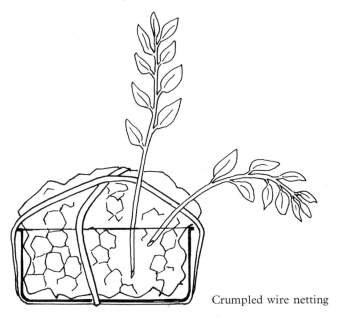

Crumpled wire netting

bought in reels but ordinary adhesive tape will serve in an emergency. If the securing bands show when the arrangement is complete, cut them away; the arrangement will hold.

3 Floral foam can also be secured in a container with tape, but it is usually better to use a foam 'anchor'. Metal ones have a lead base, rather like a pinholder, but they have long pins and only about seven or eight of them.

Small, inexpensive four-pronged plastic anchors can be bought very cheaply and one of these is quite strong enough to hold a round of foam for a low table arrangement.

The foam *must* extend above the top of the container by at least 2·5cm (1in.) so that full use can be made of the sides of the block as well as the top. Stems should be pushed in only just far enough to be held firmly, otherwise the foam is soon honeycombed and begins to break up. With care a piece can be used about three times.

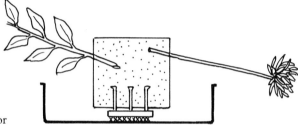

Floral foam secured with anchor

For a tall arrangement:

4 If a candlecup is to be used it should be made firm in the neck of the container with *Bostik* or *Oasisfix*, and then treated in the same way as the low bowl (3). Use the sides of the foam to give stems a downward flow, as shown in the diagram.

5 A tall vase can be almost filled with sand or gravel and a piece of foam or crumpled wire netting placed on top to protrude well above the container. Tape the foam firmly to the container, or make a cap of wire netting and secure it to the top of the vase with wire, string or tape.

Making an Arrangement Last

To get the very best and longest possible life out of an arrangement, fresh plant material needs to be given a little care and attention *before* it is arranged.

PICKING AND BUYING

Cut garden material at least two hours before you are going to arrange it and stand the stems in a bucket of deep water in a cool place, never in hot sun or by a radiator. This is usually known as 'conditioning'. Tidy up the stems as you go: remove thorns and snags, strip off lower leaves which will not be needed and any that are damaged and slit thick stems vertically for an inch or so. All flowers for arranging should be cut well before they are fully open. Bulb flowers and

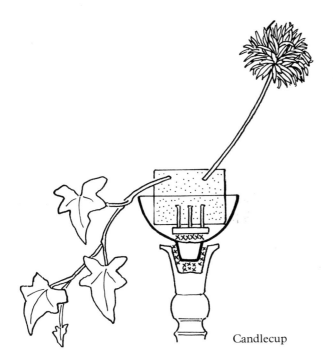

Candlecup

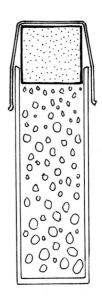

Tall vase filled with sand or gravel

roses are best cut in bud, or at least no more than half open. A fully open rose should be left on the bush, for it will not last long indoors.

The same rules apply to buying. Daffodils, iris and tulips open quickly in warm rooms so they need to be bought in bud but with a little petal colour showing. Gladioli should have only one or two florets open. Daisy-type flowers (single spray chrysanthemums, pyrethrums and Michaelmas daisies) should have greenish-yellow centres, not dark orange-brown ones, and all petals should be crisp and not ragged.

All leaves except grey ones can be plunged right under water, and two hours later will emerge crisp and clean. If plant material has been given a cool drink for two hours before being arranged, then the arrangement itself will probably last for two days longer than it otherwise would.

Aftercare
When an arrangement is complete, spray it with a misting spray such as is used for houseplants. Make sure the water in the container is topped up daily. Try to keep arrangements out of direct sun and away from fires, radiators and draughts.

Arranging in Advance for an Occasion
Flowers for any occasion can be arranged the day before, as long as they can be kept in a cool place till needed. Spray them before finally setting in place on the table.

First Aid

If by any chance an important flower or leaf has flagged (roses sometimes bend over at the neck and very young leaves can droop quickly) there are two emergency treatments worth trying:

1 Cut about 1cm (½in.) off the stem and float the flower or leaf in a bowl of luke-warm water. This breaks any air-lock and allows the stem to take up water again.

2 Wrap the flower head or spray of leaves in a cloth; cut 1cm (½in.) from the stem and plunge the stem end into about 5cm (2in.) of boiling water (yes, boiling, or as hot as you can get) for about half a minute. Remove immediately and stand or float the stem in luke-warm water for an hour or so and the flower should then be fit to return to the arrangement.

Book List

The Art of the Table, C. Herman Senn, Ward Lock, n.d.

The Book of Cut Flowers, R.P. Brotherston, T.N. Foulis, 1906

British Floral Decoration, R.F. Felton, A. & C. Black, 1910

Christmas in Williamsburg, Colonial Williamsburg Foundation, Holt, Rinehart and Winston

Définition et Règlement pour Concours Floraux, edition 1975 – published by the Belgian Flower Arrangement Society in agreement with France, Italy and Monaco

The Encyclopaedia of Judging & Exhibiting, Esther Veramae Hame'l, Ponderosa Publishers, USA, 4th ed., 1976

Everybody's Flower Book, F.M. Ramsay, Simpkin, Marshall, Hamilton & Kemp & Co., 1918

Floral Art Handbook, Royal New Zealand Institute of Horticulture, 1980

Floral Decorations à la Mode, Mrs De Salis, Longmans, Green & Co., 1891

Flower and Vase, Anne Lamplugh, Country Life, 1929

Flower Arrangements in Stately Homes, Julia Clements, George Newnes, 1966

Flower Decoration, Constance Spry, J.M. Dent, 1934

Flower Decoration in the House, Gertrude Jekyll, Country Life, 1907

Flower Decoration for the Table, Violet Stevenson, Batsford, 1964

Flowers and Food for Special Occasions, Sheila Macqueen, Ward Lock, 1980

Handbook and Show Guide for Flower Arrangers, Natal Panel of Floral Art Judges, 4th edition, 1979

Handbook for Flower Shows, National Council of State Garden Clubs, Inc., USA, 1977

Handbook of the Victorian Judges' School of Floral Art, Australia, 3rd edition

Manual of the Association of Garden Clubs of Zimbabwe, 1975

The Manual of Floral Designing, W. Cleaver Harry, De La Mare & Co. Inc., 1923

Mrs Beeton's Family Cookery, Ward Lock, 1895 and *c.* 1920

NAFAS Publications:

  A Flower Arranger's Guide to Colour Theory, 1971

  Flowers for the Table, 1978

  Handbook of Schedule Definitions, 7th edition, 1982

  Judges' Manual, 1980

  Show Guide, 1975

Party Flowers, Constance Spry, J.M. Dent, 1955

The Principles of Flower Arrangement, E.A. White, De La Mare & Co. Inc., 1926

Table Decoration, Yesterday, Today and Tomorrow, Georgiana Reynolds Smith, Tuttle, New York, 1968

Table Settings, Entertaining and Etiquette, Patricia Easterbrook Roberts, Thames & Hudson, 1967

The Wellington Plate: The Portuguese Service, Victoria and Albert Museum, 1954

The Whole Art of Dining, J. Rey, Carmona & Baker, (after 1914)

Index